THE BRITISH LIBRARY

writers' lives

Charles Dickens

~~the~~ outbreak with a violent blow upon the table as if in the heat of the moment he had mistaken it for the chest or ribs of Mr Wackford Squeers; and having by this open ~~———~~ declaration of his real feelings quite precluded himself from offering Nicholas any cautious worldly advice [~~which~~ had been his first intention] Mr Noggs went straight to the point.

"The day before yesterday"— said Newman "your ~~uncle~~ uncle received this letter. I took a hasty copy of ~~it~~ it while he was out. Shall I read it?"

"If you please"— replied Nicholas, and Newman Noggs ~~——————~~ ^according^y read as follows

· Dotheboys Hall.
"Thursday Morning

"Sir

"My pa requests me to write to you. The doctor considering it doubtful whether he will ever recover the use of his legs which prevents his holding a pen.

"We are in a state of mind beyond everything, and my pa is one ~~of~~ mask of ~~his bruises~~ brooses ~~both~~ blue and green likewise two forms are steepled in his goar. We were kimpelled ~~to has~~ him carried down into the Kitchen where he now lays. ~~~~ ~~————————~~ ~~———————~~ ~~————~~

THE BRITISH LIBRARY
writers' lives

Charles Dickens

ELIZABETH JAMES

OXFORD

UNIVERSITY PRESS

 Contents

⬱ *Early Childhood 1812–22*

Charles Dickens was born on 7 February 1812, at Mile End Terrace in the Landport area of Portsmouth. It was a Friday, a day he came to see as especially significant, a 'lucky' day for new beginnings. His parents, John and Elizabeth, were a young, lively, easy-going couple who had moved to the area on their marriage in June 1809, to be near the docks where John was employed as a clerk in the Navy Pay Office. They already had a daughter, Frances Elizabeth (Fanny), born in 1810, and a further four children were to survive infancy – Letitia, born in 1816, Frederick (1820), Alfred (1822) and Augustus (1827).

Little is known about the Dickens family. John Dickens was brought up at Crewe Hall in Cheshire, where his father was steward and his mother housekeeper. She was an extremely capable woman, recalled only dimly by her grandson as an 'unsympathetic old personage, flavoured with musty dry lavender', but fondly remembered by the Crewe children as a compelling storyteller, with a remarkable gift for 'extemporising fiction for the amusement of others'. Charles's mother, Elizabeth, was the pretty, vivacious daughter of Charles Barrow, a senior official in the same navy department as her husband. Ostensibly a respectable, middle-class family, in 1810 the Barrows were shocked to discover that their father had been found guilty of embezzling funds from the Pay Office and had fled abroad to escape prosecution.

John and Elizabeth's marriage began happily enough. John's career was progressing steadily during the tense years leading up to and immediately following the Napoleonic Wars, and after 1812 there was additional financial help from Elizabeth's widowed sister, Mary Allen, who came to live with the family. Although they were constantly on the move – Dickens failed to recognise his birthplace when he returned to Portsmouth fifty years later during one of his reading tours – this period provided pleasant memories of a small front garden, where he would trot about after his little elder sister while a nurse watched over them through a low kitchen window. Here, too, he remembered being carried downstairs to peep at the guests at a New Year's Day party, and his vivid impression of 'a very long row of

Opposite page:

Some places in England and France associated with Dickens, and (inset) a map of Dickens's London.

7

Charles Dickens

Dickens's birthplace at
Mile End Terrace,
Portsmouth, as it
is today.

Portsmouth County Council

Opposite page, above:

Portrait of Elizabeth
Dickens by J. F. Gilbert.
According to one
acquaintance, 'a great
deal of Dickens's genius'
was inherited from
his mother.

Charles Dickens Museum,
London

Opposite page, below:

Portrait of John Dickens
by Edwin Roffe, from
F. G. Kitton Charles
Dickens by Pen and
Pencil (1890). Despite
his father's failings,
Dickens always regarded
him with affection,
confessing later 'the
longer I live, the better
man I think him'.

The British Library,
Tab.440.b.7

ladies and gentlemen sitting against a wall, all drinking at once out
of little glass cups, like custard-cups'.

In 1815 John Dickens was temporarily recalled to
London, only to be transferred again two years later, first
to Sheerness, and then to Chatham in Kent, where
there had been a royal dockyard since Elizabethan
times. This busy town on the river Medway, nestling
between rich corn fields and hop gardens to the south,
and the bleak, sea-swept marshes to the north, with the
quiet cathedral town of Rochester a mile or two to the
west, was to be the family home for the next five years. It
filled Dickens's imagination, appearing again and again in
his novels, stories and essays, a 'dream of chalk and
drawbridges, and mastless ships, in a muddy river, roofed like
Noah's arks', the streets overflowing with 'soldiers, sailors, Jews, chalk,
shrimps, officers, and dockyard men' and the 'delicious' smell of tobacco smoke
pervading the air.

The Dickens family's new home was 2 (now 11) Ordnance
Terrace, a pleasant three-storey building on the edge of town,
overlooking the fields around Fort Pitt and the harbour
below. The neighbours included an affluent retired tailor,
whose widow appeared as the 'old lady' in one of
Dickens's early sketches; a crusty but well-meaning
former naval officer; and William Stroughill, a
successful plumber and glazier. It was a desirable
location for a clerk with an income of £300 a year, who
liked to think of himself as a gentleman and enjoyed a
comfortable, if somewhat extravagant, lifestyle. For
Charles this was a period of intense happiness, filled with
memories of birthday parties and summer days spent playing
with his much-loved sister Fanny, and George and little Lucy
Stroughill in the hayfield opposite the house.

Like many children at the time, five-year-old Charles received his first lessons from his mother, and like the hero of his novel, *David Copperfield*, obviously enjoyed learning the alphabet at her knee, puzzling over the fat black letters in the primer and admiring the 'easy good-nature of O and Q and S'. 'His first desire for knowledge and his earliest passion for reading were awakened by his mother,' wrote his friend and biographer, John Forster. 'She taught him regularly every day for a long time, and taught him he was convinced thoroughly well.' According to Mary Weller, one of the family servants during this period, he was 'a terrible boy to read' even at a very early age, poring over favourite picture books such as *Jack the Giant-Killer*, *Little Red Riding Hood* and *The Dandies' Ball*. A little later he and Fanny were sent to a dame school, situated above a dyer's shop and, as he recalled in one of his speeches, presided over by a formidable old woman 'who to my mind ruled the world with the birch'.

In the evenings the children listened to stories. One nursemaid, he particularly remembered, took a 'fiendish' delight in terrifying him with ghoulish tales about Captain Murderer, who chopped his wives into pies, or Tom, a glaring-eyed cat that prowled about at night 'sucking the breath of infancy'. Although Dickens may have exaggerated for literary effect – the account appears in one of his 'Uncommercial Traveller' essays – these were uncomfortably vivid images for a sensitive boy who was haunted by bad dreams throughout his childhood, and beyond. 'If we all knew our own minds,' he concluded, '... I suspect we should find our nurses responsible for most of the dark corners we are forced to go back to, against our wills.' In time, he began to create his own stories, and Mary Weller later described impromptu entertainments in the kitchen when Charles, already a clever mimic, would 'sing, recite and perform parts of plays', accompanied by Fanny on the piano. They were encouraged in these displays by their father, who would take them down to Chatham's famous Mitre Inn to sing duets, and be rewarded with applause and treats. It was about this time, Dickens recalled, that they tasted their first oyster – 'a remarkable sensation!'

The theatre, and popular amusements of all kinds, had an early and immediate attraction for Dickens. When still very young he was taken to the Theatre Royal in Rochester to see productions of Shakespeare's *Macbeth* and *Richard III*, and popular

Opposite page:

2 Ordnance Terrace, Chatham, where Dickens enjoyed the happiest years of his childhood.

Charles Dickens Museum, London

pieces such as Lillo's *George Barnwell*. Writing more than thirty years later in *Household Words*, he could still feel the excitement of the first visit to that 'sweet, dingy, shabby' little theatre: 'The green curtain, with a hole in it, through which a bright eye peeped … Our intense, fear-striken admiration of the heroine, when she let her back hair down, and went mad, in blue … The funny man (there never was such a funny man) in a red scratch wig who, when imprisoned in the deepest dungeon beneath the castle moat, sang a comic song about a leg of mutton … The final fall of the green curtain, followed by the aromatic perfume of orange-peel and lamp-oil …'. Most of all, he relished the pantomimes, often performed on make-shift stages at travelling fairs, with acrobats and harlequins in dazzling colours; but there were also treasured memories of Christmas outings to London theatres, especially to see the famous pantomime actor and clown, Grimaldi, 'in whose honor I am informed I clapped my hands with great precocity'.

As he grew older Charles was able to spend more time with his father. Whenever possible he would accompany him to the dockyard, where he never tired of watching the rope-makers and shipwrights at their work. It was here, amidst the pungent smell of sawdust, oakum and canvas, that he heard the songs of the blacksmiths and glimpsed the silent lines of convict labourers with 'great numbers on their backs as if they were street doors' described so vividly in *Great Expectations*. On special occasions he and Fanny were taken for sailing trips on board the *Chatham*, a splendid old naval yacht used for dockyard business along the Medway. At other times he and his father spent happy hours exploring the countryside around Rochester, where one of their favourite walks took them past Gad's Hill Place, an imposing country house which he always remembered his father telling him he might live in one day if he worked hard.

Early in 1821 Dickens left his dame school to attend the Classical, Mathematical and Commercial School run by William Giles, the well-educated son of a Baptist minister. Here the 'handsome boy, with long curly hair of a light colour', as he was remembered by the schoolmaster's sister, quickly attracted attention and under his kind teacher's careful guidance began to do well in his studies. Although he was not strong and suffered from severe attacks of renal colic, particularly at moments of stress, Dickens clearly enjoyed these schooldays with their friendships and games of cricket. Above all, he discovered a passion for literature, reading over and over again a small collection of cheap reprints his father had left abandoned in an attic room. Works such as *Robinson Crusoe*, *Don Quixote*, the *Arabian Nights*, *Tales of the Genii*, and the novels of Fielding and Smollett opened up new worlds far beyond his everyday experience and continued to delight him for the rest of his life.

By this time John Dickens, who had been borrowing heavily, was in serious financial difficulties, and during the summer of 1821 the family was forced to move to a smaller house in a rougher part of town near the dockyard. A year later he was recalled to Somerset House in London, and this idyllic period came to an abrupt end. For a few weeks Charles stayed behind with the Giles family until he too had to leave, travelling alone in a stagecoach with his few possessions and a copy of Goldsmith's *The Bee* which his schoolmaster had given him as a parting gift. He never forgot the dismal journey, nor the smell of the damp straw 'in which I was packed – like game – and forwarded'. 'There was no other inside passenger,' he wrote bitterly many years later, 'and I consumed my sandwiches in solitude and dreariness, and it rained hard all the way, and I thought life sloppier than I had expected to find it.'

~ *London 1822–27*

Charles arrived in London to find the family living at 16 Bayham Street, a 'mean small tenement, with a wretched little back-garden abutting on a squalid court'. In 1822 this was still a relatively rural area between Somers Town and Camden Town, where speculative builders were just beginning to erect houses for London's growing population. Grass still grew through the paving stones and there were sheep and cows in the surrounding fields, but to the nine-year-old boy, familiar with the rolling, open countryside, it seemed 'as shabby, dingy, damp, and mean a neighbourhood, as one would desire not to see'.

The troubled atmosphere at home increased his sense of desolation. John Dickens, whose expansive but volatile personality was perfectly captured in the character of Mr Micawber, was proving quite incapable of managing his mounting debts. Although money was somehow found to enroll eleven-year-old Fanny at the newly opened Royal Academy of Music, no arrangements were made to send Charles to school. To his dismay, his parents seemed not to care that he had no friends and nothing to do except run errands, clean his father's boots, and generally make himself useful about the house. As he later confided to Forster, he had always found his father kind and loving, but 'in the ease of his temper, and the straitness of his means, he appeared to have utterly lost at this time the idea of educating me at all, and to have utterly put from him the notion that I had any claim upon him, in that regard, whatever'.

Covent Garden was London's fruit, flower and vegetable market from 1670 until the early 1970s. For Dickens, it was an endlessly fascinating place of 'past and present mystery, romance, abundance, want, beauty, ugliness, fair country gardens and foul street gutters, all confused together'. Painting by Phoebus Levin, 1864.

Museum of London

George Cruikshank

In his neglected and lonely state Charles looked forward to visits to his uncle, Thomas Barrow, who lodged with a bookseller's widow in Soho, and his godfather, Christopher Huffam, a successful shipwright on the Thames at Limehouse. Both were kind to the small boy, lending him books, giving him birthday presents, and applauding his performances of the popular songs he had learned at Chatham. The journeys across London were full of interest and excitement, and he soon developed what was to become a lifelong fascination with the vibrant street-life of the city. Even at this early age he loved to explore the lively area around the Strand and Covent Garden, but he was especially drawn to Seven Dials, a notoriously unsavoury maze of narrow passages lined with gin shops and dingy, straggling houses, teeming with 'squalid', half-naked children. 'Good heavens!' he would exclaim to Forster, 'What wild visions of prodigies of wickedness, want and beggary arose in my mind out of that place.'

By the end of 1823 the family finances were in a desperate state. With her husband facing bankruptcy, Elizabeth Dickens reluctantly came to the conclusion that it was time for her to 'do something', and so, with the encouragement of Christopher Huffam, she decided to open a school. Yet more money they could ill afford was spent on renting an elegant new house on Gower Street, near Euston Square (now part of the site occupied by University College Hospital), a brass plate was fixed to the door, and circulars were distributed throughout the neighbourhood. But, according to Charles, no one ever came to school; 'nor,' he added, 'do I recollect that anybody ever proposed to come, or that the least preparation was made to receive anybody'. Instead, they were pursued by increasingly persistent creditors

Hungerford Stairs, 1822 by George Harley and Denis Dighton. Warren's Blacking Warehouse, where Dickens worked between 1824 and 1825, was the building to the right of the stairs.

Guildhall Library

Charles Dickens

'No words can express the secret agony of my soul'. *Frederick Barnard's evocative illustration for the Household Edition of Dickens's works captures the drudgery of life in the blacking factory. Reproduced from F. G. Kitton,* Charles Dickens by Pen and Pencil *(1890).*

The British Library, Tab.440.b.7

who would congregate in the street outside, shouting insults. Gradually the household furniture was sold and Charles was given the melancholy task of pawning the family's portable possessions, amongst them his father's precious collection of books which was taken, little by little, to a drunken bookseller on the Hampstead Road. Before long the house was empty except for two rooms where the family camped, as best they could, night and day.

At this critical moment Joseph Lamert, a family connection and the manager of a shoe-blacking factory, offered to employ Charles at a salary of six or seven shillings a week. The proposal was eagerly accepted, and on 9 February 1824 – two days after his twelfth birthday – he presented himself at Warren's Blacking Warehouse, a ramshackle, rat-infested building beside the river at 30 Hungerford Stairs. The work was little more than drudgery: from morning to night he was employed in sealing and labelling the pots of black paste, his only companions the rough, uneducated boys in the workroom. They were not unkind to 'the young gentleman', as they nick-named him – one, called Bob Fagin, looked after him most carefully when he suffered one of his painful attacks of colic – but as an adult Dickens could find no words to express the 'secret agony of my soul as I sunk into this companionship; compared these every-day associates with those of my happier childhood; and felt my early hopes of growing up to be a learned and distinguished man crushed in my breast'.

In later years he could not remember how long he spent at the factory – probably six months, possibly as much as a year – yet this short period had a profound and lasting effect on his life and work. It was not unusual for children of his age to have to earn a living, and his parents may have felt that a family business offered security and good prospects, but Dickens had always assumed that he was destined for something better – certainly, he had never thought of himself as a labouring child. He was shocked and deeply wounded by the experience, and ultimately bitterly angry. 'It is wonderful to me,' he confided to Forster, 'how I could have been so easily cast away at such an age … No one had compassion enough on me – a child of singular abilities, quick, eager, delicate and soon hurt, bodily or mentally – to suggest that something might have been spared, as certainly it might have been, to place me at any common school.'

The final humiliation came soon enough. Shortly after Charles began work, John Dickens was arrested for debt and taken to the Marshalsea Prison in Southwark, just south of the River Thames. In order to save money, Elizabeth and the three youngest children went to live with him there, and, once they had grown used to the formidable high walls topped with iron spikes, welcomed the relative peace and stability of the prison routine. Charles was found lodgings with an intimidating old lady who was later to become the inspiration for the 'marvellous ill-favoured, ill-conditioned' Mrs Pipchin of *Dombey and Son*. Left to fend for himself, he wrapped his shillings into little parcels, one for each day, and lived mainly on bread and cheese, with a slice of unappetising boiled pudding for dinner. 'When I had money enough I used to go to a coffee-shop, and have half-a-pint of coffee and a slice of bread and butter,' he told Forster. 'When I had no money I took a turn in Covent Garden market, and stared at the pineapples.' Life would have been intolerable but for Sundays, when he and Fanny trudged six miles to spend the day with their parents and the other children in the Marshalsea.

At the end of May 1824 John Dickens was released from prison under the Insolvent Debtors' Act. With the help of a legacy from his mother, who had died a few weeks earlier, he was able to pay off some of his creditors and gradually rebuild a precarious home life for the family, moving from one small rented house to another. It seemed to be taken for granted, however, that Charles would continue at the blacking factory; according to his own account, relief from his hopeless situation came only when his father quarrelled with Joseph Lamert, perhaps because he could no longer bear the thought that his eldest son should be engaged in such menial work. Elizabeth Dickens tried to intervene, but her husband was now determined that Charles should leave the factory and resume his education. Dickens never forgave his mother for her cruel indifference to his feelings. 'I do not write resentfully or angrily, for I know how all these things have worked together to make me what I am,' he declared quietly to Forster many years later, 'but I never afterwards forgot, I never shall forget, I never can forget, that my mother was warm for my being sent back.'

This bitter episode in his young life was not mentioned within the family again. Dickens himself did not confide in anyone until he wrote his autobiographical fragment for Forster more than twenty years later, and although it seems likely that he then showed what he had written to his wife, he never discussed it with his children. Yet it haunted his work in sly references to blacking bottles, blacking brushes and advertisements; in the piteous lives of Jo, Smike, and the many poor, lonely and neglected characters of the novels; and in the deep concern he described in one of his letters for 'all creatures who appeal through their helplessness to our gentleness and mercy … children most especially'. Dickens himself was both hardened and strengthened by the experience. As Forster noticed, it left him acutely sensitive to criticism, but also fiercely self-reliant and determined – to the extent that, in later life, he could appear harsh and even aggressive to those who did not know him well.

Wellington House Academy, where he spent the next two years, had a good reputation locally, although this is not the impression given by its fictional portrayal as Salem House in *David Copperfield*. The headmaster – 'by far the most ignorant man I have ever had the pleasure to know' – tyrannized over the staff and pupils, but Charles, like David, set himself to make the most of his new schooldays. Fellow pupils recalled a handsome, healthy-looking boy dressed in well-worn, pepper-and-salt-coloured trousers and jacket, but with a general air of smartness and unusual confidence for his age. He was quick and well read, and friends remembered his enthusiasm for amateur theatricals, his love of penny magazines and storytelling. It was a period of light-hearted freedom when he could once again enjoy boyish pleasures, keeping white mice hidden in his desk, playing practical jokes and games of all kinds. By March 1827, when his father once again ran out of money and he had to be taken out of school, Dickens was ready 'to begin the world'.

 *Apprentice Years 1827–36*

Now aged fifteen, Dickens was found work as a junior clerk in a lawyer's office belonging to a family acquaintance, situated in the heart of London's legal district around Holborn and Chancery Lane. It soon proved 'a very little world, and a very dull one'. Copying documents, routine record keeping, and running errands left him with plenty of time to explore the surrounding streets, and absorb the 'mouldy, earthy-smelling' atmosphere of the courts. During quiet afternoons when he appeared to have little to do except amuse himself by dropping cherrystones on the hats of passers-by, he delighted colleagues with his extraordinary gift for mimicry. One recalled that 'He could imitate, in a manner that I have never heard equalled, the low population of the streets ... in all their varieties, whether mere loafers or sellers of fruit, vegetables, or anything else.' After work, just like the brash young clerks in *Pickwick Papers*, he and the other 'office lads' would club together for a supper of smoked sausages and ale, or visit one of London's many theatres or places of popular

Staple Inn, Holborn, as it appeared in 1884. The buildings, squares, streets and alleyways of London's legal district around Holborn were well known to Dickens, who lived and worked here as a young man, and drew on them repeatedly for his novels.

The British Library, K.T.C.106.b.3

entertainment. Occasionally they stayed out well into the night, and many years later he was still able to recall a particularly 'grotesque' evening of eating, drinking and smoking when he 'began to doubt the mildness of the Havannahs, and to feel very much as if he had been sitting in a hackney carriage with his back to the horses'.

Despite the easy conviviality of this period, Dickens was already looking around for a more rewarding career. As soon as he reached his eighteenth birthday in February 1830 he enrolled as a reader at the British Museum, determined to make up for the inadequacies of his education. He began to teach himself shorthand in the hope of becoming a parliamentary reporter for the newspapers, at that time a popular and well-paid occupation for ambitious young men. In less than a year he had mastered the subject sufficiently well to set himself up as a freelance law reporter, transcribing proceedings in the sleepy, antiquated group of courts known as Doctors' Commons, but it was tedious and uncertain work, and he had little patience with the endless delays and complexities of the law. For a time, he confided to Forster, he even considered the stage as an alternative career, visiting the theatre almost every night to study the best acting and modelling himself, in particular, on the comedian and character actor Charles Mathews. In the spring of 1832 he went so far as to apply to Covent Garden for an audition, but a cold prevented him from keeping the appointment and he was never tempted to reapply. Much later, however, when he was appearing in his own amateur productions, and still more when he began to give dramatised readings of his novels, critics noticed the influence of Mathews on his performance. According to his eldest son, Dickens was 'a born actor'.

It was sometime during 1831 that Dickens at last made his way into the press gallery of the House of Commons, first as an occasional reporter for the *Mirror of Parliament*, a weekly journal edited by his uncle John Henry Barrow, then for the *True Sun*, a radical evening paper, before finally joining the staff of the *Morning Chronicle*, one of the leading daily newspapers. He soon became known for the speed and accuracy of his reporting, despite the uncomfortable working conditions. 'I have worn my knees by writing on them on the old back row of the old House of Commons,' he recalled in one of his speeches, 'and I have worn my feet by standing to write in a preposterous pen in the old House of Lords, where we used to be huddled together like so many sheep.' The debates he had to cover night after night during the years he was employed in the gallery – on the Reform Act of 1832, the Factory Act of 1833, the Poor Law Amendment Act of 1834 – dealt with some of the most significant social changes of the period, yet he was disappointed by what he scornfully described as a political pantomime 'particularly strong in clowns'. 'I am sufficiently behind the scenes to know the worth of political life,' he wrote in *David Copperfield*. 'I am quite an infidel about it, and shall never be converted.'

His chief companion during these dull apprenticeship years was Henry Kolle, a young bank clerk, and it may have been through Kolle that Dickens met Maria Beadnell, the pretty little dark-haired daughter of a Lombard Street banker. He fell passionately in love, later admitting that for almost four years the intensity of his feelings for her 'excluded every other idea from my mind'.

At first Maria welcomed his attentions, but he was by no means her only suitor and she clearly enjoyed playing one off against another – and in any case her parents did not approve of young 'Mr Dickin', as they called him, nor his improvident father. Gradually her feelings cooled, and after suffering 'many displays of heartless indifference' and sleepless nights spent hopelessly wandering up and down outside her house, he finally brought their relationship to an end shortly after his twenty-first birthday. For him it had been far more than mere adolescent infatuation, and there is no doubt that he was deeply hurt by her rejection – so deeply, in fact, that when he came to write the story of David Copperfield's love for Dora almost twenty years later, he found the 'scent of a geranium leaf' or a glimpse of a 'straw hat and blue ribbons' could still bring back painful memories of his own first love.

Pretty, coquettish Maria Beadnell as visualised by the American illustrator, Edmund Henry Garrett.

The British Library, 10902.ee.8

Dickens's immediate reaction was to throw himself into work, more determined than ever to make a success of his life. He began to write during the parliamentary recess that summer, and his first publication – a comic tale entitled 'A Dinner at Poplar Walk' – appeared in the *Monthly Magazine* in December 1833. When he saw his work in print he could scarcely conceal his delight: 'I walked down to Westminster Hall, and turned into it for half an hour, because my eyes were so dimmed with joy and pride that they could not bear the street, and were not fit to be seen there.' This was followed by other similar short pieces, all published anonymously until, with the second instalment of 'The Boarding House' in August 1834, he signed himself 'Boz' for the first time. This was an abbreviation of the family nickname for his youngest brother, Augustus, who was called Moses after a character in Goldsmith's *The Vicar of Wakefield* – 'which being facetiously pronounced through the nose became Boses, and being shortened became Boz'.

That summer Dickens was invited to join the staff of the *Morning Chronicle* at a salary of five guineas a week, employed as much for his 'faculty for descriptive writing' as his reporting skills. The editor, John Black – 'my first hearty out-and-out appreciator' – saw to it that he was not confined to routine parliamentary work, but encouraged to write reviews and sketches, and at the same time given the opportunity to cover important meetings, dinners and election campaigns throughout the country. Dickens responded with enthusiasm, relishing the excitement of galloping through the night in a carriage, hastily scribbling his copy by the light of a swaying lantern, the mud flying in through the open windows as he wrote. He treated himself to a new blue cloak with black velvet trimmings, the corner of which he was observed to wear stylishly thrown over one shoulder 'à l'Espagnole'; he grew his hair long and began to indulge a taste for fancy waistcoats. Later that year, when his father was once more in serious financial difficulties, he paid off some of the debts, settled his mother and the younger children into cheaper lodgings, and then moved himself and his fourteen-year-old brother, Fred, into rented chambers in Furnival's Inn, just off Holborn.

Still not quite twenty-three, Dickens was now independent, with a growing reputation as a talented reporter. Early in 1835 he came a step closer to achieving literary success when he was invited to contribute a series of twenty 'street sketches'

The earliest known portrait of Dickens, painted by his aunt, Janet Barrow, in 1830.

Charles Dickens Museum, London

Charles Dickens

Dickens's work as a parliamentary reporter often meant he had to work extremely long hours, much to Catherine's evident disappointment. In this letter, written at three in the morning shortly after their engagement in May 1835, he assures her of his 'love which nothing can lessen – an affection which no alteration of time or circumstance can ever abate'.

The British Library, Add. MS 43689, f.7

Brompton

3 O'Clock – Tuesday.

My ever dearest Kate:

If our little conversation at last night, have presented itself to your mind at all, since I left you, I hope it has only been to remind you of my repeated and solemn assurances of entertaining for you a love which nothing can lessen – an affection which no alteration of time or circumstance can

In this letter of 20 January 1835 to George Hogarth, editor of the Evening Chronicle *and Dickens's future father-in-law, Dickens respectfully proposes a series of sketches in return for 'some additional remuner-ation'. When these were published as the first series of* Sketches by Boz, *Hogarth wrote an enthusiastic review, praising Dickens as 'a close and acute observer of characters and manners, with a strong sense of the ridiculous…'.*

The British Library, Add. MS 29300, f.105

to the *Chronicle's* newly-founded sister paper, the *Evening Chronicle*. With an increase of two guineas a week in his salary, he was now on the way to becoming a professional author, and it was as a promising young star that George Hogarth, the paper's editor, welcomed Dickens to his home in Brompton. Before long he was a regular guest at parties and musical evenings, thoroughly enjoying the warmth and gaiety of the large family circle and delighting everyone with his comic songs, practical jokes and sheer vitality.

Catherine Hogarth, the eldest daughter, was nineteen when they met; her sisters Mary and Georgina were fourteen and seven. Catherine was a pretty girl, if rather plump, with 'large, heavy-lidded blue eyes', a slightly turned-up nose, 'small, round and red-lipped' mouth, and a 'genial smiling expression'. Most people who came to know her described her as 'sweet-natured' and 'kind', with a quiet sense of fun, and if she seemed placid, even passive, at times, Dickens was soon happily in love. They became engaged in May 1835, but this time he remained firmly in control of the relationship and of his emotions. His work was increasingly demanding, and in letter after letter during their engagement he apologised for having to cancel or postpone his evening visits, urging her to keep cheerful, not to be 'coss' or peevish, and to remember that 'I have never ceased to love you for one moment, since I knew you; nor shall I'.

Dickens's first book, a revised and expanded collection of his newspaper pieces, was published by John Macrone on 8 February 1836. *Sketches by Boz*, with illustrations by the well-known artist George Cruikshank, was an immediate success; a second edition appeared in August, and a second series – containing a further twenty tales and sketches – in December. In later years he was inclined to dismiss the work as 'crude and ill-considered', but, as Forster observed, it provided a dazzling picture of 'everyday London at its best and worst, in its humours and enjoyments as well as its sufferings and sins'. Within days Dickens had been approached by a new publishing firm, Chapman and Hall, with an offer of £14 a month to provide the text for a series of sporting illustrations by the artist Robert Seymour, which they proposed to issue in shilling instalments. It was not what he had in mind – he was already working on an opera libretto and a farce, and had ideas for more sketches and a three-volume novel – but Catherine and he were now planning to marry, with all the expense of setting up home. 'The work will be no joke,' he wrote to her on 10 February, 'but the emolument is too tempting to resist.'

By the early nineteenth century, part publication or publication in instalments, which had begun as a way of spreading the cost of a book, was chiefly associated with illustrated works or crudely printed series of the classics. 'My friends told me it was a low, cheap form of publication,' Dickens recalled, 'by which I should ruin all my rising hopes …'. Instead he quickly found he had stumbled upon a new and immensely popular method of publishing fiction, which enabled him to reach the widest possible audience. It became the pattern for most of his future work, with nine of his novels appearing in monthly instalments; soon the thirty-two-page parts, with their distinctive coloured wrappers and lively illustrations, were a familiar sight in the bookshops.

Portrait of Catherine, Dickens's wife, painted two years after their marriage, by Samuel Laurence, in 1838.

Charles Dickens Museum, London

The first number of *Pickwick Papers* appeared on Thursday 31 March 1836, traditionally known as 'magazine day' in the booktrade. Two days later, on 2 April, Dickens and Catherine were married at St Luke's Church in Chelsea, where the novelist Charles Kingsley's father was vicar. It was a quiet ceremony attended only by their close families, John Macrone, and the best man, Thomas Beard, one of Dickens's oldest friends. Henry Burnett, Fanny Dickens's fiancé, recalled that the bride looked bright and pleasant, 'dressed in the simplest and neatest manner'. After a simple wedding breakfast the couple spent a short honeymoon in the quiet village of Chalk, not far from Rochester, before returning to a larger, 'tastefully' furnished, set of chambers in Furnival's Inn. There Mary Hogarth found her sister 'as happy as the day is long' when she visited later that month; Dickens, however, was once more hard at work.

Pickwick made slow progress at first: sales of the opening numbers were surprisingly low, and the book attracted little attention. To make matters worse, Seymour, already a disappointed and troubled man, committed suicide before he had completed the plates for the second number; it proved difficult to find a replacement, even though Chapman and Hall agreed to increase the amount of text in proportion to the number of illustrations. This effectively put Dickens in charge of the project, and he was probably responsible for choosing Hablôt K. Browne, a shy, amenable young man, to illustrate the rest of the work. They quickly formed an excellent partnership (Browne actually adopted the name Phiz 'to harmonise ... better with ... Boz') which lasted for over twenty years.

The fourth number of *Pickwick*, the first to contain illustrations by Browne, also introduced the character of Sam Weller, an engaging cockney who immediately struck a chord with the public. The *Metropolitan Magazine* described it as 'the best that has yet appeared'; by the time the fifth number was published, with its hilarious account of the Eatanswill election, the press was reporting that Boz had 'completely taken possession of the ear, and the heart too, of his countrymen', and there were stories of crowds standing with their noses flattened against the booksellers' windows, eager to catch a glimpse of the latest instalment. Chapman and Hall increased Dickens's fee to £25 a month as sales continued to rise – to 14,000 copies in February 1837, then 26,000 in June, reaching nearly 40,000 by the time the last number appeared in November.

Opposite page:

Hablôt K. Browne was unknown when he was engaged to illustrate Pickwick Papers, *but it marked the beginning of his successful career. After Dickens's death, although partially crippled in his right hand, Browne redrew his illustrations, including the famous 'First appearance of Mr. Samuel Weller', for the Household Edition of the novels.*

British Museum, 1969-9-22-1-11

34

By then this rollicking tale, which owed so much to the picaresque novels of Smollett, Sterne and Fielding, was a sensation. Its irrepressible good humour, touched with pathos and understanding, charmed everyone – rich or poor, young or old. Office boys and apprentices enjoyed it as much as country ladies and clergymen; a Liverpool locksmith and his friends devoured each new instalment as eagerly as eminent judges and doctors in London. There were Pickwick hats and canes, cigars and chintzes; there were song books and jest books, adaptations and

The White Hart, one of London's old coaching inns and the setting for Mr Pickwick's meeting with Sam Weller.

The British Library, K.T.C.106.b.3

37

Charles Dickens

During the weekend of his first wedding anniversary in April 1837 Dickens moved to 48 Doughty Street. Built in the eighteenth century but the only one of his London homes still standing, it is now the Charles Dickens Museum.

Photograph by Ken Price

Opposite page:

Pickwick Papers was published in monthly parts between March 1836 and November 1837, each with a green cover decorated with sporting scenes by Seymour. This set of the parts, exhibited at the Festival of Britain Exhibition in 1951, is a particularly fine copy.

The British Library, Dex. 270

continuations; the rotund, bespectacled figure of Mr Pickwick and the cheerful 'Wellerisms' of Sam were recognised and repeated everywhere. 'I did not think there had been a place where English was spoken to which "Boz" had not penetrated,' Miss Mitford, the author of *Our Village*, wrote to a friend in Ireland. At the age of twenty-five, in the memorable words of one reviewer, Dickens had been catapulted to fame 'like a rocket'; he was already 'the inimitable Boz', blessed with a popular appeal which was to last for the rest of his life.

~ *The Inimitable Boz 1837–42*

Old houses in Jacob's Island, Bermondsey, painted by John Wykeham Archer in 1855. Jacob's Island, described as a desolate, disease-ridden stretch of land 'surrounded by a muddy ditch, six or eight feet deep ... when the tide is in', was the scene of Bill Sikes's death in Oliver Twist.

British Museum, 1874-3-14-347

Success drew Dickens into a frenzy of activity. He told friends he was 'over head and ears with work', but this did not stop him from agreeing, in November 1836, to edit a monthly magazine for the publisher Richard Bentley, even though he was already committed to writing further novels. For this he was to be paid £20 a month, with an additional twenty guineas for his own contribution to each issue – far more than he was receiving from Chapman and Hall, and enough to enable him to give up his position with the *Morning Chronicle*. He hoped that his new task would be 'less burdensome', not least because he was now facing additional domestic responsibilities: on 6 January 1837 Catherine gave birth to their first child, also called Charles and promptly hailed as 'the Infant Phenomenon' by his proud father.

Dickens's second novel, *Oliver Twist*, was written for serialization in *Bentley's Miscellany*. It began as a journalist's scathing attack on the New Poor Law, which replaced the old system of local parish relief for the poor and destitute with a brutal, impersonal workhouse regime, but as he warmed to his subject memories of his own childhood misery, hunger and loneliness came flooding back. With a newborn baby at home, he threw his 'whole heart and soul' into the harrowing story of an innocent child's struggle for survival in the violent and nightmarish world of the crowded slums of London. The theme was not new: 'The Parish Boy's Progress' of the subtitle was familiar from the work of Hogarth and the eighteenth-century satirists, and the crude juxtaposition of good and evil was typical of much popular theatre and penny literature, but many of Dickens's readers were startled by the sombre tone and his obvious fascination with the lives of criminals and outcasts. Some tried to dismiss the book as the latest in a long tradition of 'Newgate novels', popular fiction based on the lives

Cut-out characters and scenery for a toy theatre version of Oliver Twist. *Such adaptations and spin-offs were an indication of the immense popularity of Dickens's early work.*

The British Library, Dex. 313(5)

In his carefully worded preface to the Cheap Edition of Oliver Twist, *published in 1850, Dickens responded to critics who suggested that places such as Jacob's Island existed only in his imagination by renewing his attack on the slum dwellings of the poor.*

The British Library, Dex. 289

of criminals; some, like Lord Melbourne, were disgusted by its portrayal of low life, especially the sympathetic treatment of the prostitute, Nancy; others, however, noticed the author's exceptional ability to create characters so full of 'living feelings and passions ... that they immediately become visibly, personally and intimately known to us'. Significantly, perhaps, Dickens insisted that the novel should be advertised and published under his own name when it appeared in book form, and critics began to compare him, not with his contemporaries, but with Shakespeare and Sir Walter Scott.

In April 1837 Dickens, Catherine and the baby moved to 48 Doughty Street – a 'frightfully first-class Family Mansion' – but they had scarcely begun to enjoy the comfortable new surroundings when their lives were shattered by the sudden death of Catherine's sister, Mary Hogarth. From the earliest days of their marriage Mary had been a frequent and very welcome visitor, joining the young couple in 'merry banterings around the fire' and charming their friends with her sweet, affectionate nature. One evening in May, when they had all been to the theatre together, Mary suddenly collapsed; they watched over her anxiously through the night but she died a few hours later in her brother-in-law's arms, aged just seventeen.

Dickens was devastated. He suffered another of the excruciatingly painful attacks in his side which had so troubled him as a child, and for the only time in his career found himself unable to write his monthly instalments; he took a ring from her finger and wore it on his own, he kept a lock of her hair, and for months afterwards he dreamed about her every night. Almost a year later he wrote in his diary, 'We never know the full value of blessings 'till we lose them ... but if she were with us now … sympathising with all my thoughts and feelings more than any one I knew ever did or will – I think I should have nothing to wish for, but a continuance of such happiness.' It was an intensely emotional response, and in some respects he never recovered from the loss which came when they were all so young and carefree. In Forster's words, Mary became 'the ideal of his life' – a good, gentle girl whom he said he loved as a dearest sister, yet with 'the fondest father's pride'. Inevitably, her death also had a profound influence on his work, reflected in the heart-rending descriptions of sick and dying children in his novels, and the idealised portraits of characters such as Little Nell, who remain trapped between childhood and maturity in a fairy-tale state of innocence.

    The tragedy left an emptiness in the little household which made the company of friends all the more important. Dickens liked nothing better than to get up a party for a morning's ride to Hampstead or Richmond, or an afternoon walk through the city streets; when he was working these excursions helped him to relax and to think, and he would often say that he needed exercise to stimulate his imagination. Among the most frequent visitors to Doughty Street was the historical novelist W. H. Ainsworth, who introduced Dickens to a Bohemian circle of artists and writers, including the painter Daniel Maclise, the celebrated Shakespearean actor William Macready, and – most important of all – John Forster. Forster and Dickens had much in common: they were the same age, both came from lower-middle-class backgrounds, and both had tried to make a career in the law but turned instead to journalism and literature. They also shared the same high spirits, love of the theatre, dinners and good company, and although Forster could be opinionated and overbearing, he was a loyal and devoted friend to Dickens throughout his life.

The only surviving image of Mary Hogarth, Dickens's beloved sister-in-law, copied from a posthumous portrait by Hablôt K. Browne. Dickens thought it 'worthless' as 'a record of that dear face'.

Charles Dickens Museum, London

John Forster (1812–76) and Dickens were close friends by the time Daniel Maclise made this sketch in May 1840. Forster advised Dickens on his business affairs and read the manuscripts and proofs of most of his novels. Although they saw less of each other in their later years, Forster's biography (published in three volumes in 1872–74) provides a unique record of Dickens's life.

Victoria and Albert Museum

It was to Forster that Dickens turned when he realized that he needed help with his business affairs. In the excitement following his sudden rise to fame he had committed himself to an impossible schedule of work, and for sums which were beginning to seem derisory, given that 'Boz' was so much in demand. He was determined to free himself from these hasty agreements, which involved all three of his publishers but chiefly centred on Bentley, who was equally reluctant to lose his most profitable author, especially when he had the law on his side. Months of increasingly acrimonious discussions eventually provoked Dickens into giving up his editorship of *Bentley's Miscellany* in January 1839, and subsequently severing all relations with the man he had come to see – not entirely fairly – as the 'Burlington Street brigand'. There were to be many such quarrels in the years ahead, but for the time being all his novels (including the *Miscellany's* advertised new serial, *Barnaby Rudge*) were entrusted to Chapman and Hall, who had behaved so generously over *Pickwick Papers* and were already contracted to publish his next novel, *Nicholas Nickleby*.

Dickens has often been criticised for an excessively mercenary attitude to his work. The truth was that, as a professional author with no other source of income, he had a living to earn; but he was also a shrewd businessman who knew enough about the life of a struggling writer to realise that it could lead to grinding poverty, especially for those who did not look after their copyrights. As he complained to Forster in 1839, writing was often hard and wearisome, and 'the consciousness that my books are enriching everybody connected with them but myself … while for those who are nearest and dearest to me I can realise little more than a genteel subsistence … puts me out of hearts and spirits'. And his family commitments were growing: his eldest daughter, Mary (Mamie), was born in March 1838, followed by Kate, the most spirited of all his children, in October 1839. Meanwhile his father was becoming even more of a burden, continually running up debts and borrowing money on the strength of his famous son's name, and his brother, Fred, was showing ominous signs of having inherited their father's weakness of character, especially in financial matters.

Nicholas Nickleby, Dickens's third novel, was published in monthly instalments between March 1838 and September 1839. It was intended to be 'of a similar nature' to *Pickwick Papers*, with the emphasis on cheerful merriment and 'kindliest sympathies', but, like *Oliver Twist*, quickly developed a strong strand of social criticism. The brutality of cheap boarding schools in North Yorkshire, which operated as little more than detention centres for unwanted children, was a long-standing scandal which Dickens now decided to investigate for himself. The conditions he found during an exploratory visit with Hablôt Browne in January 1838 were bad enough to convince him 'that the rascalities of those Yorkshire schoolmasters cannot easily be exaggerated'. He based Dotheboys Hall on Bowes Academy, run by William Shaw, who had been prosecuted fifteen years earlier for ill-treating his pupils, in the hope of drawing attention, once and for all, to these horrific establishments. The result could not have been more satisfactory – within ten years of the novel's publication all of these schools had been closed down.

Yet *Nicholas Nickleby* was much more than a successful piece of social satire. Readers were immediately enthralled by the brilliant comedy of the Squeers family, the pathos of Smike's tormented life, and the exotic vitality of the theatrical

Charles Dickens

Crummleses, while Dickens himself – now writing with unprecedented fluency – became increasingly absorbed in their adventures. Sales of the first number reached an astonishing 50,000 copies, prompting a stream of cheap imitations and unauthorised dramatic adaptations which only added to the demand. In the United States the novel was serialized by the firm of Carey, Lea and Blanchard, who sent their agent to negotiate for early proofs, even though the absence of an international copyright agreement meant that they were under no obligation to pay for the rights to reproduce British books. Publication of the final instalment, after a period of intense concentration during which Dickens's diary records just one word – 'Work', was marked by a 'splendid' dinner, and the unveiling of Maclise's portrait of Dickens at his writing desk. Engraved by William Finden, this formed the frontispiece to *Nicholas Nickleby* when it was published in volume form, and has since become one of the most famous images of the author (see page 2).

Dickens was now the leading writer of the day, fêted by London society, a member of two of the most prestigious gentlemen's clubs, the Garrick and the Athenaeum (to which he was elected at the same time as Charles Darwin), and increasingly in demand as a public speaker. In 1841 the citizens of Edinburgh gave a dinner in his honour and made him a freeman of the city – a 'brilliant' occasion for a young man still in his twenties, which he proudly remembered as 'the first public recognition and encouragement I ever received'. He met and became friends with well-known literary men of the day such as Leigh Hunt, Walter Savage Landor, Samuel Rogers, and the influential editor and lawyer Lord Jeffrey, and, although some people were put off by his 'vulgar' bursts of loud laughter and dandified dress, there were many more who recognised his sharp intelligence. 'He is a

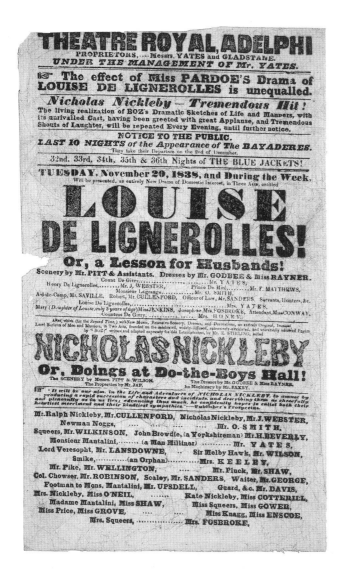

Many poor people knew Dickens's work, not from reading his novels, but from seeing dramatizations at the popular theatres of the day. Nicholas Nickleby *was still being written when Edward Stirling's adaptation opened at the Adelphi Theatre, London, on 19 November 1838.*

The British Library, Dex. 316

fine little fellow,' wrote the historian Thomas Carlyle soon after their first meeting, '… a face of the utmost *mobility* … a quiet, shrewd-looking little fellow, who seems to guess pretty well what he is and what others are'.

 Success enabled Dickens to move from Doughty Street to 1 Devonshire Terrace, a grand Georgian house near Regent's Park, meticulously furnished with paintings, mirrors, ornaments and a library of more than two thousand books. Here he loved to play the host at lavish dinner parties, often ending with a gin punch he concocted himself, followed by a riotous evening of parlour games, charades or dancing. Summers were usually spent at Broadstairs in Kent – the 'favourite old-fashioned watering-place' of one of his essays – where friends were frequently invited to join the family party. In these more relaxed surroundings he could be wildly exuberant, and one nineteen-year-old visitor remembered how they were dancing a quadrille at the end of the jetty one evening when Dickens suddenly

1 Devonshire Terrace, London, where Dickens and his family lived from 1841 to 1851, photographed by H. S. Ward and C. W. B. Ward in the early 1900s. The house was demolished in 1960.

The British Library, 10350.ee.9

dragged her into the sea, ruining her silk dress. The same girl noticed that, for all his good spirits, his parents seemed slightly restrained in his presence as if they were afraid of offending him; in certain moods, she recalled, his eyes could flash like 'danger-lamps' and then even his children would avoid him.

Critics have often pointed out that something of the same manic quality can be seen in his next work, *The Old Curiosity Shop*, in which the character of Quilp reflects certain aspects of Dickens's own personality. It was conceived as 'a little child story' for *Master Humphrey's Clock*, a new literary magazine he had persuaded Chapman and Hall to publish, but sales declined so sharply when readers discovered that it did not contain the expected new novel by their favourite author that he was forced to expand his original idea into a full-length serial. Writing in weekly instalments, he found, was exhausting: 'Mr. Shandy's Clock was nothing to mine – wind, wind, wind, always winding am I; and day and night the alarum is in my ears, warning me that it must not run down.' He worked without a break throughout 1840, deliberately reopening old wounds as he approached the death of Little Nell, and finishing the final chapters at four in the morning one day in the middle of January 1841. 'It makes me very melancholy to think that all these people are lost to me for ever,' he told Forster the next day. 'I feel as if I never could become attached to any new characters.'

In fact he plunged immediately into *Barnaby Rudge*, the long-delayed novel which had been promised to Bentley. The story was set during the anti-Catholic Gordon Riots of the 1780s, but the underlying themes of violence, madness and disorder had a darker contemporary resonance in the recent Poor Law uprisings and militant public demonstrations of the Chartist movement for political reform. It was not an easy subject, and at first Dickens confessed that he struggled to find inspiration, 'wandering about the most wretched and distressful streets' of the city. He was not well, his father was once again running up debts in his name, and he was afraid that the public was tiring of his work. By September 1841 he had not only convinced himself that he needed a break, but that he should seize the opportunity to visit America, where *The Old Curiosity Shop* had been greeted with enormous enthusiasm. With Forster's support he managed to persuade Chapman and Hall to allow him a year's leave, during which they would pay a monthly retainer of £150 in

*At Dickens's suggestion,
Master Humphrey's
Clock was illustrated
with wood engravings
'dropped into the text'.
Hablôt K. Browne's
striking picture of Quilp
leaning out of the
tavern window is
carefully positioned so as
to complement the words
on the page.*

*The British Library,
Dex. 267*

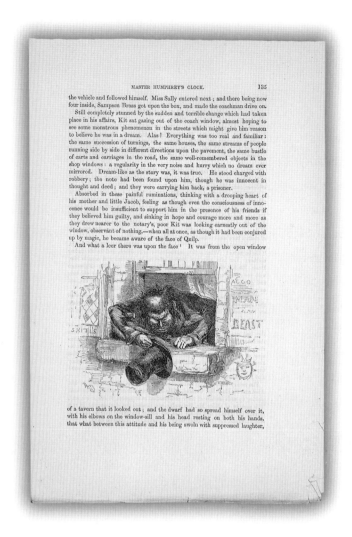

return for an eventual half-share in the copyright of his next novel; a 'little book' about his travels was something of an afterthought, but this, too, was finally agreed.

Once everything was settled the very thought of the trip made him feel better; even a painful operation for an ulcer did not trouble him for long. 'I am in an exquisitely lazy state,' he wrote from Broadstairs, 'bathing, walking, reading, lying in the sun, doing everything but working … haunted by visions of America, night and day.' Little could he know that his daughter Kate, in her own old age, would look back on these years at Doughty Street and Devonshire Terrace as the happiest of her father's adult life: 'Those were the days of domestic happiness, the days before inside and outside influences evolved and brushed away the sweetness of life – while his face was yet pale and unlined …'.

~ *America 1842–44*

Charles and Catherine Dickens sailed from Liverpool on 4 January on board the steamship *Britannia*. For comfort during their six months' absence, they took with them Catherine's maid, the ever-reliable Anne Brown (whom Dickens described as 'a moral cork jacket' – their lifesaver), and a delightful sketch of the children by Maclise which was given pride of place in their room wherever they stayed. The children themselves, including the eleven-month-old baby, Walter, were left in the charge of Fred, with help from Catherine's fourteen year-old sister, Georgina, and under the general supervision of the Macreadys.

After a wretched voyage during which they were all extremely seasick, they arrived in Boston to a tumultuous welcome. Even before the ship had safely docked Dickens was surrounded by newspaper editors, all clamouring to meet him, while a huge crowd congregated on the wharf. It was just the beginning of a breath-taking succession of dinners, receptions, visits and stimulating new experiences which he

The Britannia, *one of the Cunard line's first steamships, on which Dickens sailed to America in 1842. Engraved for the frontispiece of the Cheap Edition of* American Notes *(1850) after a water-colour by Dickens's friend, the marine artist Clarkson Stanfield.*

The British Library, 012614.a.53/7

Charles Dickens

described with almost incredulous enthusiasm in long letters home. People lined the streets whenever he went out; they cheered him at the theatre, deluged him with messages of congratulation; they besieged the hotel, he complained jokingly to Maclise, so that Catherine and he were forced to hold court 'like a kind of Queen and Albert'; they even thronged the entrance to the artist's studio where he went to have his portrait painted. The sober Bostonians had seen nothing like it, and according to one observer were almost relieved when their exuberant young guest moved on to Hartford and New Haven. In New York the highlight of their visit was the lavish 'Boz Ball', where Dickens and his wife were paraded twice round the vast, glittering ballroom to acknowledge the cheers of over 3,000 guests.

At first he found much to admire in his welcoming hosts, and their impressive country. He enjoyed meeting most of the eminent public and literary figures, including Longfellow, Washington Irving, Edgar Allen Poe, the historian W. H. Prescott, and the Harvard classicist Cornelius Felton – 'one of the jolliest and simplest of men ... not at all starry, *or* stripey' – with whom he quickly struck up a warm friendship. He praised the beauty and elegance of Boston, and was fascinated by the bustle and colour of New York, where the crowded pavements seemed to be 'polished' with the tread of feet until they shone. He was quick to acknowledge the frank, courteous and hospitable nature of the American people. Yet as the weeks went by the strain of being constantly in the public eye began to tell on him. By the time they left New York Dickens was desperate for peace and privacy, and homesick for the children, 'the study, the Sunday's dinner ... anything and everything connected with our life at Home'. As they journeyed south to Philadelphia, Washington, Richmond, west to Louisville and St Louis, and north to Cincinnati he found the extremes of climate uncomfortable, and the travelling by rail, boat and rough roads increasingly exhausting. Like many English visitors, he disliked the overheated buildings and was revolted by the 'odious practices' of chewing tobacco and spitting. He was horrified by the dehumanising regime of solitary confinement at the Eastern Penitentiary in Philadelphia, and profoundly detested slavery, feeling such an acute 'sense of shame' throughout their stay in Maryland and Virginia that he quickly abandoned any plans to travel further south.

Most of all, he was angered by America's refusal to sign an international copyright agreement, which meant that a British author, however popular, and regardless of whether he had an arrangement with an American publisher, could not protect his works from piracy. He found it insulting, not to say hypocritical, that a country which had welcomed him so extravagantly could still condone a situation that prevented him from receiving fair payment for his American editions. As an honoured visitor, he was warned that it was not tactful of him to urge his case so firmly; even so, he was startled by the furious outcry and recriminations which greeted every attempt he made to raise the matter. Derided by the cheap press as a 'low-bred, vulgar man' for preferring 'dollars and cents to literary fame', and 'a flash waistcoat to a laurel wreath', he soon became convinced that there was less freedom of speech on this subject in America than in any other country 'on the face of the earth'.

The final month of their stay was spent in Canada, where at last he felt able to relax. To their 'unspeakable delight' Dickens and Catherine had Niagara Falls to themselves, and were free to ramble about in their oldest clothes, 'walk ankle-deep in the mud and thoroughly enjoy ourselves'. They both took part in amateur theatricals with the officers at the British garrison in Montreal – Catherine, to his great surprise and pleasure, playing 'devilish well' – and then they were on their way home. Arriving in London on 29 June, a day earlier than expected, Dickens was overjoyed to be with his friends and children again; never had he appreciated his home so keenly, he wrote to Jonathan Chapman in Boston, as on that evening.

If Dickens was disappointed by 'the Republic of my imagination', he had learned some valuable lessons about himself, his country and the responsibilities of fame. These were the hungry forties, and Britain was in the grip of a severe trade depression. He began to take a more serious interest in political and social questions, writing letters to the press, attending charity dinners (even though he said he did not much care for them), chairing committees, organising subscriptions to raise funds, and making speeches. He wrote an impassioned defence of Lord Ashley's Mines and Collieries Bill, which sought to prohibit the employment of women and children underground, and vowed to deliver a 'sledge hammer' blow against the employment of children, often as young as five or six, in factories. He enlisted the help of the heiress Miss Angela Burdett Coutts, who shared his instinctive sympathy and concern for the poor, becoming her unofficial advisor and a trusted friend. On her behalf he visited the Ragged School at Saffron Hill in Clerkenwell (the miserable, disease-ridden location for Fagin's den in *Oliver Twist*), where he was horrified to find three dilapidated rooms filled with filthy and unruly street urchins. What he saw convinced him

that it was pointless trying to teach creeds and catechisms to the starving who did not even know the difference between right and wrong; something much more radical was urgently needed. 'I ... am as sure as it is possible for one to be of anything which has not happened,' he wrote, 'that in the prodigious misery and ignorance of the swarming masses of mankind in England, the seeds of its certain ruin are sown.'

The books which followed his visit to America reflected this new seriousness. After all the controversy, *American Notes* – his first major work of non-fiction – was eagerly awaited on both sides of the Atlantic. He carefully avoided any mention of international copyright, dwelling instead on the country's social institutions and systems, but although the book sold well during the autumn of 1843, the critics were predictably hostile. Even Forster later admitted that it had none of the freshness and charm of Dickens's letters. *Martin Chuzzlewit*, the novel he began almost immediately and dedicated to Miss Coutts, was more carefully considered than any of his previous stories. Dickens knew that in focusing on a central theme of

'Mrs Gamp propoges [sic] a toast', one of Hablôt K. Browne's most successful illustrations, from Martin Chuzzlewit.

The British Library, C.117.d.3

A view of Cloth Fair, near Smithfield market, from a photograph taken in 1877. Decaying wooden houses, their upper storeys over-hanging narrow alleys, were still a familiar sight in Victorian London.

The British Library, Tab. 700.b.3

selfishness he was writing with greater power than ever before, yet, for all the brilliant comedy of Mr Pecksniff and Mrs Gamp, and generally favourable reviews, the book failed to capture the public imagination. Even when he transferred the action to America sales did not rise above 23,000, and Chapman and Hall went so far as to threaten to invoke a £50 penalty clause in their contract. Not surprisingly given the penetrating satire of the central chapters, American readers received the book with renewed animosity.

It was only with the appearance of the first of his Christmas books, *A Christmas Carol*, that Dickens was able to express his preoccupations in a truly popular form. Conceived during a fund-raising visit to the Manchester Athenaeum in October 1843, and written within a few weeks during which he spent many nights pacing the black London streets deep in thought, this simple tale of the miserly Scrooge's moral transformation caused a sensation. The first edition of 6,000 copies sold within a few days, but more surprisingly for a seasonal story, the demand continued long after Christmas into the early summer. Reviewers and ordinary readers all recognized the genuine goodness and humanity of the book; complete strangers wrote to tell him how it brought new enjoyment and understanding of the festival into their homes. According to the novelist William Makepeace Thackeray, it defied criticism: 'It seems to me a national benefit, and to every man and woman who reads it a personal kindness.'

Over the years Dickens was to become firmly associated with the idea of Christmas as a time of joy and benevolence, particularly through the Christmas books and special numbers of his magazines, which effortlessly captured the holiday spirit for his own and future generations. He himself loved to celebrate the season, which coincided with his eldest son's birthday on Twelfth Night. Dressed as a magician, he would make the children scream with laughter at his jokes and tricks, and their eyes sparkle as he distributed sweets and cakes 'like some good fairy'. Within days of finishing *A Christmas Carol* he was the life and soul of a party at the

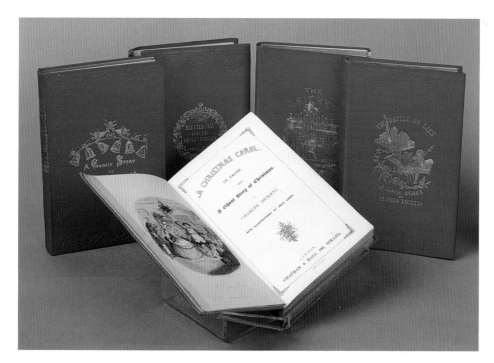

Dickens's Christmas Books – A Christmas Carol *(1843),* The Chimes *(1844),* The Cricket on the Hearth *(1845),* The Battle of Life *(1846) and* The Haunted Man *(1848) – confirmed his extraordinary popular appeal.*

The British Library, Ashley 630 and Dex. 293

William Makepeace Thackeray in 1862, painted by Samuel Laurence. Although they were never close friends, Dickens and Thackeray respected each other as fellow professionals. Thackeray, in particular, was always generous in his praise of Dickens's work.

National Portrait Gallery

Macreadys' house, playing the conjuror for a 'whole hour', Jane Carlyle recalled, until he and Forster 'seemed *drunk* with their efforts'. Afterwards he led the company in a riotous evening of country dancing, 'the pulling of crackers, the drinking of champagne, and the making of speeches', which lasted well into the early hours of the morning.

Unfortunately, despite its immense success, *A Christmas Carol* was a financial disaster for its author. Dickens had arranged for it to be published at his own expense, lavishly got up in rose-brown binding with gilt decoration and coloured endpapers, and four colour plates by John Leech. As Forster pointed out, the five shillings charged for the book was too high a price for most readers, but too low to offset the extravagant production costs. Typically, however, Dickens blamed Chapman and Hall: 'I have not the least doubt,' he wrote to his solicitor, 'they have run the expenses up, anyhow, purposely to bring me back and disgust me with charges.' This new blow left him seriously short of money, coming, as it did, so soon after the disappointment of *Martin Chuzzlewit*; it gave him, however, the perfect excuse to transfer his books to his printers, Bradbury and Evans, and to allow his thoughts to turn, yet again, to travel. Once he had convinced himself that it would be cheaper to live abroad, and that he needed rest and stimulation, he was in no mood to listen to Forster's warnings against another interruption to his work. Armed with a £2,800 advance from his new publishers, and with only a second Christmas book to write, he purchased an old, lumbering coach – 'about the size of your library,' he announced gleefully to Forster – and on 2 July 1844 set out in high spirits for Genoa. They were quite a 'caravan' – Catherine, her sister Georgina, who was by now an accepted part of the family, five children (including the latest arrival, the six-month-old baby Francis), three servants, their French guide Louis Roche, and Timber the dog.

⁓ *Europe 1844–46*

Dickens was entranced by the intense colour and heat of the Mediterranean summer. He had never seen such lilac and purple as the distant hills, or such an impenetrable blue as the sea beneath his windows: 'It looks as if a draught of it … would wash out everything else, and make a great blue blank of your intellect,' he wrote to Maclise. He soon relaxed into a leisurely regime of eating, reading and swimming, avoiding visitors whenever possible and exerting himself only enough to learn a little Italian. 'I never knew what it was to be lazy, before,' he confided to Count d'Orsay. Their house, the Palazzo Peschiere, was like an 'enchanted place in an Eastern story', situated within the city walls but set amongst beautiful gardens filled with orange and lemon trees, fountains and statues. Genoa itself, with its picturesque narrow streets and cool, dark churches, was one of the loveliest cities in Italy, although 'the gorgeous and wonderful reality' of Venice, which he visited later that year, exceeded his wildest dreams.

Yet Forster was right to be apprehensive about this Italian visit. In his biography he remarked simply that it marked a turning point in Dickens's life, during which his restlessness and indefinable 'want of something' became more apparent. At first he found it impossible to work in strange surroundings with the endless clashing of bells breaking in on his thoughts, but by the middle of October Dickens reported that he was in a 'ferocious excitement' with *The Chimes*, the most uncompromising of his Christmas books, in which he determined to 'strike a great blow for the poor'. As soon as it was finished, and despite the difficulties and cost of winter travel, he insisted on making a short visit to London to give a private reading to a specially invited group of like-minded

Dickens with Catherine and her sister, Georgina, 1843. This sketch by Maclise was greatly admired by John Forster, who considered it one of the best images of Dickens: 'He is in his most pleasing aspect; flattered, if you will; but nothing that is known to me gives a general impression so lifelike and true of the then frank, eager, handsome face.'

The British Library, Dex. 316

friends, including Thomas Carlyle, the playwright Douglas Jerrold, and the Liberal journalist Laman Blanchard. The evening was a triumph: his sympathetic listeners were moved to tears and laughter, and he had the first intoxicating hint of the powerful hold he could have over an audience. Before the end of the visit he and Forster were laying plans for an amateur theatrical group, but in the back of his mind there was now the idea that he might one day give public readings from his books.

Dickens returned to Genoa in time for Christmas celebrations, but the New Year was not very old before he found himself caught up in an episode which was to lead to his first open disagreement with Catherine. Among their neighbours were Emile de la Rue, a Swiss banker, and his English wife, an attractive young woman who suffered from a nervous disorder which resulted in headaches, nightmares and convulsions. Dickens offered to try to relieve her symptoms through mesmerism, a controversial form of hypnosis which had long interested him. With her anxious husband's agreement, during the next few months he devoted himself to his 'patient', eagerly responding to any call, whatever the time of day or night, whenever her condition appeared particularly severe. When he and Catherine left for a tour of Italy early in the spring it was agreed that the de la Rues should meet them in Rome;

meanwhile he insisted on receiving daily bulletins from M. de la Rue, and secretly promised to set aside an hour each morning to focus his attention on the 'sad invalid' in an attempt to hypnotize her by telepathy.

Although Dickens was genuinely concerned for Madame's 'recovery and happiness', and doubtless spent many pleasant hours in her company, his letters suggest that he was probably more interested in his own mesmeric powers. Certainly he was so wrapped up in his observations that he seems to have been quite unaware of the effect his obsessive behaviour was having on Catherine. Whether she sensed an underlying sexual element in the association or simply did not trust Mme. de la Rue, for once she did not try to conceal her feelings. Much to his annoyance and severe embarrassment, Dickens was forced to make excuses for her obvious antagonism, and eventually to confess something of the truth – a mortifying experience for such a proud and strong-willed man. More than eight years later he was still fiercely protesting to Catherine 'that the intense pursuit of any idea that takes complete possession of me, is one of the qualities that makes me different … from other men. Whatever made you unhappy in the Genoa time had no other root, beginning, middle, or end, than whatever has made you proud and honored in your married life.'

Catherine was left behind in Genoa when Dickens made his flying visit to London to read The Chimes *to his friends, but Maclise sent her this light-hearted sketch of the evening's 'triumphant' proceedings.*

Victoria and Albert Museum

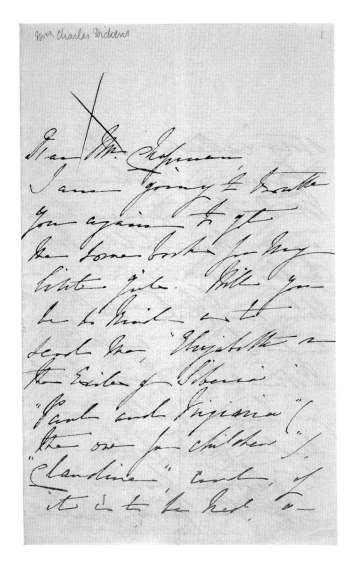

At the time Catherine was again pregnant, and possibly anxious and over-emotional as a result. She always suffered severely from post-natal depression, and continual child-bearing was beginning to affect her health and spirits, placing an inevitable strain on their marriage. An awkward tendency to trip or fall, first mentioned by her husband during their visit to America, became more noticeable over the years, probably indicating her increasing nervousness or lack of confidence. Dickens tried hard to be sympathetic and to make a joke of her accidents, but he could not always hide his irritation, nor his only partly facetious lack of enthusiasm for each new addition to the family. Their sixth child, Alfred, was born in October 1845; the seventh, Sydney, in April 1847 after a particularly difficult delivery. Following this experience, Dickens promised Catherine that she should be given chloroform for the birth of Henry in January 1849, even though its use was still highly experimental. Their third daughter, Dora, was born in 1850, and their tenth and last child, Edward (known as Plorn) in 1852. 'I am not quite clear that I particularly wanted the latter,' Dickens told William Howitt, 'but I have no doubt that he is good for me in some point of view or other.'

Catherine's sister, Georgina, who helped to look after all these children, was a very different character. Now aged seventeen – the same age as Mary had been when she died – she was lively, intelligent and strangely reminiscent of the sister whom Dickens still remembered so fondly. 'At times … when she and Kate and I are sitting together,' he told her mother, 'I seem to think that what has happened is a

Some biographers have criticised Catherine as an indifferent mother, but in this letter, written shortly before Charley went away to school in 1847, she asks the publisher Frederick Chapman to send a 'nice Bible and Prayer-Book' for him, and some books for her little girls.

The British Library, Dex. 316

melancholy dream from which I am just awakening.' Enthralled by her first experience of foreign travel, she was in high spirits throughout this Italian visit; Dickens referred to her as 'my little Pet' and seemed to think of her as another daughter as much as a sister. He enjoyed her company – she was an excellent mimic, with a sharp sense of humour – and in the years to come, especially as Catherine became more lethargic and withdrawn, it was Georgina who joined enthusiastically in his theatrical exploits, accompanied him on his long walks, helped him with his correspondence and – like Esther Summerson in *Bleak House*, for whom she might have been the model – quietly saw to the children or household affairs.

Dickens returned to London with his family at the beginning of July, and immediately plunged into preparations for a scheme of amateur theatricals which had been discussed with his friends the previous Christmas. The play chosen was Ben Jonson's *Every Man in his Humour*, in which he took the part of Bobadil, dressed in 'fiery' colours complete with elaborately curled black moustache. By all accounts the performance was no better than most amateur dramatics, and probably gave more pleasure to the actors than the spectators, but it created enough of a stir for a repeat performance to be given at St James's Theatre in aid of charity. Dickens revelled in his managerial role, organising costumes, scenery, lighting, even the playbills, and conducting rehearsals with all the seriousness of a professional theatre director. During the next ten years he organised many similar productions: he said it was like 'writing a book in company', an enjoyable change from the lonely life of a novelist, and an increasingly welcome escape from domestic responsibilities and unhappiness.

A far less satisfactory enterprise during the winter of 1845–46 was his involvement with a new liberal newspaper, the *Daily News*, a joint venture of his publishers, Bradbury and Evans, and the eminent gardener-turned-railway entrepreneur, Joseph Paxton. After some hesitation and much against the advice of friends such as Macready, Dickens accepted the post of editor, appointing some of the best journalists in London to his staff and placing his father in charge of the reporters. The first issue appeared in January 1846, amidst much speculation and excitement at the height of the Corn Laws controversy. It was an ideal moment for a radical paper, but Dickens had seriously underestimated the wearisome labour of

attending the office night after night, of supervising printers, commissioning contributions, and above all, of having to be accountable to the paper's proprietors. He resigned after just seventeen issues, leaving Forster to fulfil the rest of his contract. Although he later admitted that it had been a mistake, the experience was not entirely wasted: extracts from his travel notes, later published as *Pictures from Italy*, continued to appear, and were followed during the next few months by an outspoken series of letters against capital punishment. In the longer term it rekindled his interest in journalism, especially in managing a periodical of his own.

As soon as he was free from editorial responsibilities, Dickens decided to take his family to Switzerland, a country which had greatly appealed to him when they passed through it on their way back from Italy the previous year. They settled in Lausanne, in a 'perfect doll's house' beside the lake, where he was soon hard at work on a new serial. Beautiful surroundings, agreeable neighbours, and plenty of English visitors (including Alfred, Lord Tennyson, whose work he greatly admired) at first provided the kind of stimulation he needed, but after six months he realised that he was missing the streets and bustle of city life. 'I can't express how much I want these,' he told Forster. 'It seems as if they supplied something to my brain, which it cannot bear, when busy, to lose … The toil and labour of writing, day after day, without that magic lantern, is IMMENSE!!' It was time to move on, and by the end of November he had transported his family to Paris. It was bitterly cold, their house in the Rue de Courcelles was small and inconvenient, but immediately he felt more at home.

A view of Paris described by Dickens in one of his later stories as a crowded city of 'pure enchantment'. Illustration by Eugene Lami for Jules Janin's Un hiver à Paris *(1843).*

Bridgeman Art Library/ Musée de la Ville de Paris, Musée Carnavalet

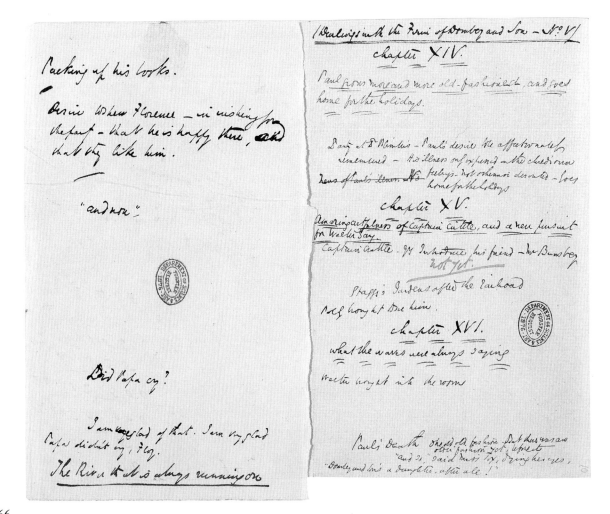 Dombey and Son *and* David Copperfield *1847–51*

Dombey and Son was published in monthly parts between September 1846 and March 1848. It had been two years since Dickens's last major novel and he was no longer the only significant exponent of what had by now become the dominant literary form of the day. Charlotte Brontë, her sisters Emily and Anne, Mrs Gaskell, Charles Kingsley and Anthony Trollope all published their first novels in 1847 or 1848, and Thackeray's *Vanity Fair*, his first serialized work, was appearing at about the same time.

For Dickens this new novel also marked an important departure. It is the first for which a complete set of his working notes survives, and from these it is possible to see how carefully he planned each number in advance, painstakingly building the plot around a central theme. The setting is contemporary; the cold, calculating pride of the self-made city merchant, Mr Dombey, dominates the story, but also represents a shamelessly ruthless and hypocritical society in which there is little room for warmth, generosity, kindness or love, and where even the closest human relationships are seen in terms of monetary value. Everything contributes towards the overall design: the deliberate contrasts between characters and scenes, pathos and comedy, the insistent symbolism of the railway and the sea are all carefully considered. Even Browne's illustrations were closely examined to ensure that they harmonised with the text, and that Dombey, in particular, should not appear too much of a caricature.

Dickens returned to England at the end of February 1847 as the death of little Paul took London and Paris by storm. 'Oh, my dear dear Dickens! what a No. 5 you have given us!' wrote his friend Lord Jeffrey. 'I have so cried and sobbed over it last night, and again this morning … Since that divine Nelly … there has been nothing like it.' Thackeray was equally generous with his praise: 'There's no writing against

This illustration from Drawings of the London and Birmingham Railway *by John C. Bourne (1839) shows the devastation caused by the construction of the Camden Town cutting, through the area described as Staggs's Gardens in* Dombey and Son. Wellington House Academy, *the school Dickens attended from 1824–26, was partially demolished in the process, but the remaining portion can be seen on the left of the picture.*

The British Library, 650.b.23

such power as this,' he is said to have exclaimed. 'It is stupendous!' Although some critics felt that the concluding numbers were disappointing, others, recognizing his 'improved experience', were quick to claim it as a triumph. With monthly sales averaging 32,000 (compared with fewer than 5,000 for *Vanity Fair*) and an approximate income of £450 from each instalment, *Dombey* was a success in every sense of the word.

Indeed after 1847, the year in which he launched the popular Cheap Edition of his works, Dickens had good reason to feel financially and professionally secure. Neatly printed in double columns with new prefaces and illustrations, and published in a range of formats from 1½-pence weekly numbers, to

7-pence monthly parts, to bound volumes in a choice of bindings, this was an enterprising scheme to tap a wide variety of new markets, and Dickens frankly expected to make 'a great deal of money out of the idea'. At the same time, he hoped that the edition – shrewdly dedicated to 'the English people' – would become, as he wrote in the carefully worded advertisement, 'a permanent inmate of many English homes, where in his old shape, he was known only as a guest, or hardly known at all'.

The years immediately following the completion of *Dombey* were crammed with activity as Dickens resumed his breathless routine of seeing friends, attending dinners and parties, organising excursions and amateur theatricals, answering letters and public speaking. As Forster observed, 'he did even his nothings in a strenuous way'. Much of his time and energy was devoted to charitable projects, especially to Urania Cottage, Miss Coutts's home for former prostitutes and other needy young women, which opened in November 1847 after years of planning. Although his

Derby Day, *1858, by William Powell Frith. Frith was a great admirer of Dickens, whom he first met in 1842. His paintings of Victorian life, in which rich and poor, flower-sellers and fortune-tellers, dandies and demure young ladies jostle side-by-side, reflect the teeming life and incident of his friend's novels.*

Tate Collections

involvement was not publicly acknowledged at the time, he was the guiding spirit behind the organization and much of the day-to-day administration of the venture.

Unlike many other similar institutions, which often failed to consider the future of their inmates, it was Dickens's intention that the women should be helped to start new lives in the colonies, where he sincerely hoped 'they will do well, marry honest men and be happy'. As he told supporters, he firmly believed that they had to be '*tempted* to virtue' with a fair and sensible regime based on 'affectionate kindness' and understanding. He advised against lecturing them for their past sins, knowing that in most cases they had already been made only too well aware of the degradation of their lives, and had an 'exaggerated dread' of the kind of dogmatic religion which he came to see as one of the worst aspects of the Established Church. On a purely practical level, he was determined to avoid 'being too grim and gloomy', choosing 'cheerful' colours for the girls' dresses and allowing time for more satisfying activities, such as the planting of flower beds during the summer. For Dickens, Christian charity was always a matter of 'active sympathy and cheerful usefulness'. 'It is through such means I humbly believe that God must be approached, and hope and peace of mind must be won,' he told one young correspondent at this time. 'The world is not a dream, but a reality, of which we are the chief part, and in which we must be up and doing something.'

Slowly and painfully during this period Dickens was beginning to come to terms with his life. Now approaching forty ('such an old man', he assured Macready shortly before his birthday in 1849), he found his mind turning increasingly to the past, especially to the days when, as he had confided to Washington Irving in 1841, he was 'a very small and not over-particularly-taken-care-of boy'. In the spring of 1847 he revealed to Forster the truth about his humiliating period as a little 'labouring hind' in the blacking factory, and, having broken his silence, found it a relief to share his memories. Over the coming months, but particularly after the death of his dear sister, Fanny, from tuberculosis in September 1848, he wrote an account of his early years, the words flowing easily from his pen as if it were an ordinary letter. Meanwhile, in his final Christmas book, *The Haunted Man*, published in December 1848, he explored his ideas about memory through the character of Redlaw, a famous chemist who has allowed his life to be blighted by dwelling too much on past injuries and sadness.

Like Dickens himself, he has to accept that good and bad are 'inextricably linked in remembrance' – that you cannot chose 'the enjoyment of recollecting only the good. To have all the best of it you must remember the worst also.'

These reflections found expression in Dickens's next novel, the most intimate and intensely personal of all his works. Inspired by a New Year's visit to Yarmouth, with its miles of bleak, featureless marshland, he began to write early in 1849 and, once he had settled on a title, was soon happily immersed in *David Copperfield*. 'I feel, thank God, quite confident in the story,' he confessed on 6 June; by July he was 'getting on like a house on fire', and in November he reported himself 'wonderfully in harness' with 'a smashing number'. The second half of the novel went equally smoothly, in spite of many other commitments during 1850. In February he was promising 'some beautiful comic love', and although for a time he was 'undecided about Dora', by July he had the story 'carefully planned' to the end. The concluding numbers were written to the 'hoarse music' of the sea at his beloved Broadstairs: 'I have been tremendously at work these two days,' he wrote as he reached the climax of the story, 'eight hours at a stretch yesterday, and six and a half today, with the Ham and Steerforth chapter, which has completely knocked me over – utterly defeated me!' At last, on 21 October he was able to report that he was 'within three pages of the shore'. 'Oh, my dear Forster, if I were to say half of what *Copperfield* makes me

Broadstairs was Dickens's favourite holiday resort from 1837 to 1851. Fort House, situated on the headland 'with the sea winds blowing through it', particularly attracted him; here he wrote much of David Copperfield *and began to plan* Bleak House.

Charles Dickens Museum, London

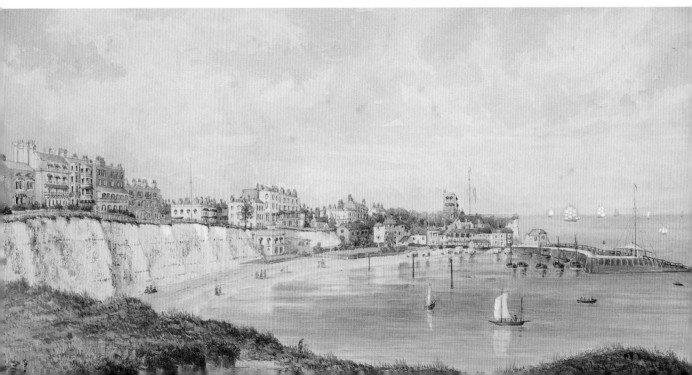

Frederick Barnard's illustration of the Yarmouth boathouse for the Household Edition of David Copperfield, *published in 1873. Barnard, who provided most of the new illustrations for this edition, is considered one of the most successful illustrators of Dickens's works.*

The British Library, 12603.h.15

feel tonight, how strangely, even to you, I should be turned inside-out! I seem to be sending some part of myself into the Shadowy World.'

The public loved it, and, although sales were disappointing at first, *David Copperfield* quickly became one of his most popular works. Dickens himself declared it his 'favourite child', knowing how much of himself he had invested in this 'very complicated interweaving of truth and fiction', filled with memorable characters who embody some of his deepest feelings about himself, his parents, his first love, life and marriage. Written entirely in the first person, it is often described as the 'heart' of Dickens, occupying not merely a central place in his affections but in his career as a writer, poised triumphantly between the buoyant optimism of his early novels and the thoughtful, deeply probing works of his later years.

Long before he had finished *David Copperfield*, Dickens had finally fulfilled his ambition to found and edit a popular magazine. In his introductory essay to *Household Words*, the title eventually chosen for the periodical, he outlined his aim to stimulate awareness and discussion of important social issues, while promising to 'tenderly cherish that light of Fancy which is inherent in the human breast'. It was published by Bradbury and Evans, who had a quarter share in the profits; Dickens himself received a half share in addition to a salary of £500 a year for his work as 'Conductor'; the remaining quarter was divided between Forster and William Henry Wills, an experienced journalist from the *Daily News*, whom he appointed as his sub-editor and business manager at a salary of £8 a week. Although he complained that Wills 'has not the ghost of an idea in the imaginative way', Dickens valued his energy and reliability, and during the twenty years of their working relationship came to depend on his friendship and discretion.

The first issue of *Household Words* appeared on 27 March 1850, priced at 2 pence. Despite its unexciting appearance and lack of illustrations, it was an immediate success, with a regular circulation of almost 40,000 copies. Within four months Dickens was predicting 'a good round profit', an optimism borne out by a total of £1,715 in the first year, providing a substantial addition to his annual income. Dickens took his editorial responsibilities seriously, soliciting contributions, answering letters, reading manuscripts (over 900 in 1852 alone), arranging material, correcting proofs and dealing with printers. He tirelessly amended, revised, condensed, reworked and rewrote articles, sometimes just 'delicately' altering a few words but more often hacking and hewing the proofs until they resembled an 'inky fishing net'. None of the contributions was signed, but Dickens's name appeared at the top of each page, and he spared no effort to ensure that the journal reflected his views and literary style.

He soon attracted a number of regular writers, among them Wilkie Collins (who was to become his literary protégé, friend and collaborator, later joining the editorial staff for a time), Mrs Gaskell, Harriet Martineau, and a group of novice journalists, including G. A. Sala, Percy Fitzgerald and Edmund Yates, often referred to as 'Dickens's young men'. Between them they supplied each issue with a selection of good literature, informative articles on subjects ranging from science to biography and domestic economy, and reports on important social issues such as housing, sanitation and education. Dickens himself contributed more than a hundred essays, including an account of Urania Cottage and one of his most beautiful pieces, 'A Child's Dream of a Star', as well as serials, stories and collaborative articles. Many of the topics reflected his own concerns and interests, often anticipating themes which found their way into his novels, but he never lost sight of his audience, nor of their need to be amused as well as informed. 'I have been looking over the back numbers,' he told Wills on one occasion. 'They lapse too much into a dreary, arithmetical, Cocker-cum-Walkingame dustyness that is powerfully depressing.' 'KEEP HOUSEHOLD WORDS imaginative!'

As always, amateur theatricals provided a welcome outlet for what Dickens called his 'superfluous steam' throughout this period, especially when they could be put to charitable purpose. In 1847, and again in 1848, he reassembled his company for a series of benefit performances, which led, in 1850, to the formation of the Guild of Literature and Art, an ambitious scheme proposed by the successful novelist Edward Bulwer Lytton to provide pensions and housing for needy artists and writers who might otherwise be dependent on charity and patronage. In November 1850 a revival of *Every Man in His Humour* was presented at Knebworth, Bulwer Lytton's Hertfordshire home, but for the formal launch of the Guild in 1851 – the year of the Great Exhibition – it was decided that Bulwer Lytton would write a new comedy for the company to perform in London. After months of time-consuming correspondence ('about … equal to the business of the Home Office,' complained Dickens) and feverish preparations, the first night of *Not So Bad As We Seem* took place on 16 May at the palatial Piccadilly residence of the Duke of Devonshire, in the presence of Queen Victoria and Prince Albert. With the set designed by the versatile Joseph Paxton and a cast which included Wilkie Collins, the illustrator John Tenniel and the painter Augustus Egg, as well as Dickens himself, it brought together a remarkable display of talent (even though the dramatist, Douglas Jerrold, joked that they were 'a great deal worse than we ought to be'). Public performances were given in the elegant Hanover Square Rooms in London's West End during the summer, followed by a series of extremely popular provincial tours, culminating in a triumphant evening in front of a cheering audience of 1,200 at Sunderland on 28 August 1852.

The excitement was timely. For all its hectic achievement this period was not without its troubles, and Dickens was glad of the distraction from a succession of personal cares which clouded the early months of 1851. Catherine was slow in recovering from Dora's birth in August 1850. Exhausted and worried about the fragile baby, by the following spring she was obviously very ill, suffering from severe headaches, giddiness and confusion. After consultation with his doctor, Dickens placed her in the care of a specialist at the popular spa town of Malvern, to undergo a 'rigorous discipline of exercise, air and cold water'. It was while he was anxiously commuting between

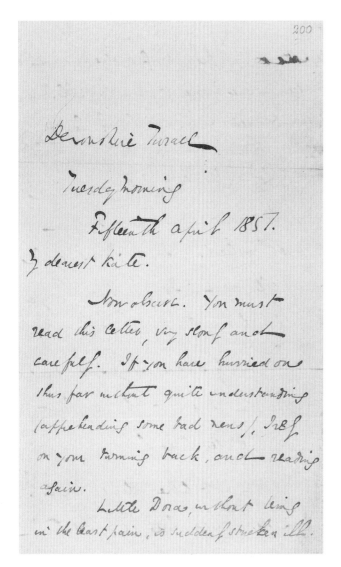

Malvern and the *Household Words* office in London that he was shocked to hear his father was seriously ill following a horrific operation (performed without anaesthetic) on his bladder. For a few days it seemed that John Dickens might rally, but he died – 'O so quietly' – on 31 March. In the bleak days and nights which followed Dickens restlessly paced the streets of London, suddenly overwhelmed by the 'whole battle' of life. Barely two weeks later he was in London again for a dinner in aid of the General Theatrical Fund when news was brought to him that little Dora, whom he had been nursing just a few hours earlier, had died unexpectedly. All night he sat beside her tiny body, then in the morning he wrote a tender, thoughtful message for Forster to take to Catherine in Malvern, preparing her for the sad news she would have to face when she returned to London: 'You must read this letter, very slowly and carefully,' he wrote. 'You would suppose her quietly asleep. But I am sure she is very ill … I do not – why should I say I do, to you my dear! – I do not think her recovery at all likely.'

Catherine bore her grief bravely, but she was desperately low and badly in need of rest and a change of surroundings. Dickens rented Fort House in Broadstairs for the summer, and decided to let their Devonshire Terrace home until September, when the lease was due to expire. Meanwhile he tried various ploys to distract her attention, and it was probably for this reason that he published a light-hearted little cookery book, entitled *What Shall We Have for Dinner?*, under a theatrical pseudonym for Catherine in October 1851. Whenever possible he used the excuse of house-hunting to take her out, eventually deciding upon Tavistock House in Tavistock Square – their last home together.

~ *Darkening Days 1852–56*

Tavistock House was an imposing five-storey building, set back from the square behind an iron railing. It was in a dismal, dilapidated condition when Dickens took over the lease, and he spent the autumn busily overseeing extensive renovations, as usual supervising every detail from the installation of new plumbing (he always insisted on starting each day with a cold shower), to the choice of carpets and wallpaper, and the transformation of the garden. According to the artist and illustrator Marcus Stone, Dickens's passionate – almost fanatical – 'love of order and fitness' was felt all over the house, in the tasteful hanging of the pictures, the neat

A view of The Strand, a street familiar to Dickens from his earliest days in London, and where the publishers, Chapman and Hall, had their offices.

Museum of London

Hablôt K. Browne, Dickens's principal illustrator from 1836 to 1860, in later life. From an engraving by F. W. Pailthorpe.

The British Library, Dex. 157

furnishing of the girls' room with its two little iron bedsteads covered in pretty chintz, even down to the orderly row of pegs in the hall for the boys' hats and coats. With the children in mind he set aside a large room on the first floor which could be used for parties or transformed into the 'smallest theatre in the world' for family entertainments, especially on Twelfth Night.

Overlooking the square was Dickens's spacious study, separated from the drawing-room by sliding doors fitted with imitation bookshelves. When closed they appeared part of the book-lined walls; when opened out he was able to pace up and down the length of the house, deep in thought. A large mahogany-framed mirror hung on one wall, and beneath the window was his desk, carefully laid out each morning with a vase of fresh flowers, a supply of paper, pens and his customary blue ink. By now he had a well-established routine, which was followed with business-like regularity every day with only very rare exceptions.

He got up at seven, breakfasted at eight and shortly after nine would retreat to his study, where he remained, undisturbed and in absolute silence, until lunchtime. Between two and five in the afternoon he went out for a brisk walk through the countryside or the streets of London, often still engrossed in his work, his eyes looking straight ahead but missing nothing. Dinner was at six, and he would spend the evenings with family or friends before retiring to bed around midnight. As he explained to one correspondent at this time, his whole life was arranged 'according to the system that experience has shewn me to make my work easiest and happiest'.

Although he rarely spoke about his writing, those who were closest to Dickens knew how thoroughly it filled his soul and his imagination. His daughter Mamie once described a period of convalescence during the Tavistock Square years, when she was allowed to lie quietly on a sofa in her father's study. 'Suddenly he jumped up from his chair and rushed to a mirror which hung near, and in which I could see the reflection of some extraordinary facial contortions he was making. He returned rapidly to his desk, wrote furiously for a few moments, and then went again to the mirror.' Throughout the morning, she recalled, he carried on muttering to himself and acting out the scenes he was writing, not only quite oblivious of his surroundings but totally absorbed in the characters he was creating. To his eldest son it seemed as though he lived two lives, 'one with us and one with his fictitious people, and I am equally certain that the children of his brain were much more real to him at times than we were'. As for Dickens himself (who once complained that a popular novel he had been reading appeared to have been written 'by somebody who lived next door to the people, rather than inside of 'em'), he was becoming more than ever convinced that all art 'must be imbued with human passions and action'.

At last the refurbishment of Tavistock House was finished, and in November Dickens was able to start work on the novel which had been 'whirling' through his mind during the autumn, and was to occupy his attention throughout 1852 and much of the following year.

> *London. Michaelmas Term lately over, and the Lord Chancellor sitting in Lincoln's Inn Hall. Implacable November weather. As much mud in the streets, as if the waters had but newly retired from the face of the earth, and it would not be wonderful to meet a Megalosaurus, forty feet long or so, waddling like an elephantine lizard up Holborn Hill …*
>
> *Fog everywhere. Fog up the river, where it flows among green aits and meadows; fog down the river, where it rolls defiled among the tiers of shipping, and the waterside pollutions of a great (and dirty) city. Fog on the Essex marshes, fog on the Kentish heights …*

The sombre tone of Bleak House *was matched by Browne's 'dark plates', produced by a printing process specially developed to create a shaded impression. 'Tom All Alone's' with its view of a filthy alley leading to a graveyard, represented many London streets of the time.*

The British Library, Dex. 287

The familiar opening paragraphs of *Bleak House*, written at a time when he was most acutely aware of the need for reform, set the scene for his first sustained attack on contemporary British institutions. No longer content to criticise individual abuses, he now demonstrated how the whole of society, from the rich to the poor, the strong to the weak, is drawn together in a slow but irresistible cycle of destruction and decay. The suffocating London fog is a symbol of the impenetrable confusion of the country's legal system, represented by the Court of Chancery with its interminable lawsuit of Jarndyce and Jarndyce; the rain falling on silent Chesney Wold suggests the ineffectual isolation of the political establishment. Both are associated with despair and injustice which infect every aspect of life, from the misguided philanthropists who devote their lives to the distant people of Africa while neglecting their families and the poor around them, to the illiterate, downtrodden masses who can see no way out of their misery. And somehow linking them all is sad, suffering Jo, the little crossing sweeper who is hustled and jostled and continually moved on until he believes himself to 'have no business, here, or there, or anywhere'. The story ends with paralysis, death and shame, and the ominous presence of Inspector Bucket, the first detective in English fiction. It was a far cry from the early novels in which Dickens had cheerfully set out to entertain his readers. 'Pray do not … be induced to suppose that I ever write merely to amuse, or without an object,' he now told one critic of *Bleak House*. 'Without it, my pursuit – and the steadiness, patience, seclusion, regularity, hard work, and self-concentration it demands – would be utterly worthless to me.'

Bleak House sold well, but the tremendous labour involved, at the same time as editing *Household Words*, helping Miss Coutts with her charities, and the usual round of public and social engagements, left Dickens feeling ill and exhausted. As a change from Broadstairs, which had become intolerably noisy in recent years, he took Catherine, Georgina and the children to Boulogne for the summer of 1853, a 'bright, airy, pleasant, cheerful town' which he was to visit many times in the future. The pretty Chateau des Moulineaux, and its wonderfully kind and generous owner, Monsieur Beaucourt-Mutuel, soon restored his spirits, and by October he was busily finalising plans for an extended tour of Switzerland and Italy with Wilkie Collins and the painter Augustus Egg. Restless and energetic as ever, he whisked his two companions from Lausanne to Chamounix and the Mer de Glace, across the Simplon pass and overnight to Milan, down to Genoa for an exhaustive tour of his old haunts, then crammed them onto an overloaded steamer to Naples, and so to Rome, Florence and Venice for a relentless round of sight-seeing. The trio got on well together; Wilkie Collins, in particular, twelve years Dickens's junior and an easy-going, colourful character who lived his unconventional life to the full, was by now a good friend and ideal company on a carefree holiday.

Wilkie Collins (1824–89), aged thirty-seven, photographed by Herbert Watkins. Despite the difference in their ages, he and Dickens became close friends, colleagues and literary collaborators. Dickens recognised and encouraged Collins's talent: 'I was certain,' he once told him, 'that you were the Writer who would come ahead of all the field – being the only one who combined invention and power, and that profound conviction that nothing of worth is to be done without work.'

The British Library, Dex. 70

On his return to London in December Dickens immediately set about preparing a series of readings he had agreed to give in aid of the Birmingham and Midland Institute, a recently founded educational organisation for working men. By now he was used to reading extracts from his works to groups of friends, but this was the first time he had performed for a public audience and he was apprehensive about his ability to recreate the same intimate atmosphere in a large hall. He need not have worried. Within a few moments, he reported, '... we were all going on together ... as if we had been sitting round the fire'. His reading of *A Christmas Carol* on 30 December for 2,500 working people, at reduced prices, was a triumph: 'They lost nothing, misinterpreted nothing, followed everything closely, laughed and cried ... and animated me to that extent that I felt as if we were all bodily going up in the clouds together.'

This visit was much in his mind as he began his next novel early in the new year of 1854. He had not intended to start another book so soon, but the sales of *Household Words* had fallen so sharply during his absence the previous autumn that Bradbury and Evans begged him to write a new serial especially for the magazine. The idea of *Hard Times*, Dickens later revealed to a friend, 'laid hold of me by the throat in a very violent manner'. Although he had often thought of writing a novel with an industrial setting, the long-running strike of cotton workers in Preston, now into its fourth month, encouraged him to explore his deepening concern about the gulf between employers and employees, and the vital importance of imagination and entertainment, especially in the lives of the poor. The theme was particularly suited to *Household Words*, but he found it very difficult to compress the story into short weekly instalments; the effort of continually paring his text gave him 'perpetual trouble', and he was often tired and 'dreary'. He wrote the final chapters in Boulogne, telling Forster that 'I am three parts mad, and the fourth delirious, with perpetual rushing at *Hard Times*'; by the time he had finished he felt utterly 'used up'.

For all that, the novel was a financial success. Its serialization between 1 April and 12 August 1854 more than doubled the circulation of the magazine, and the volume – appropriately dedicated to Thomas Carlyle – sold surprisingly well. The critics, however, were confused or dismissive, and for many years it remained one of Dickens's most controversial books, famously denounced as 'sullen socialism' by

Macaulay but praised by John Ruskin in 1860 as the greatest of Dickens's works, to be studied carefully by everyone interested in social questions. George Bernard Shaw noticed the greater seriousness of tone with approval: 'Many readers find the change disappointing. Others find Dickens worth reading for the first time,' he wrote. '*Hard Times* was written to make you uncomfortable; and it will make you uncomfortable … though it will perhaps interest you more, and certainly leave a deeper scar on you, than any two of its forerunners.'

In the months following publication of the novel – aptly retitled *Hard Times for These Times* for the volume edition – Dickens's anger and frustration intensified. Yet another outbreak of cholera in London during the hot summer of 1854, and more and more damning revelations about government mismanagement of the Crimean War, prompted a stream of hard-hitting articles in *Household Words*. Although he had often been invited to stand for Parliament he had always refused in the belief that he could do more good by his writing, and now he lost no opportunity to attack the complacent indifference, incompetence and hypocrisy of the country's politicians. 'Any half-dozen shopkeepers taken at random from the London Directory and shot into Downing Street out of sacks' could have managed things better, he wrote in May 1855, the month he joined his friend Austen Henry Layard's short-lived Administrative Reform Association. In fact Dickens never lost his old contempt for 'the national cinder-heap', as he had recently branded the House of Commons in *Hard Times*, but by this time he was beginning to feel that 'representative government is become altogether a failure with us'. If only the people would rouse themselves to peaceful protest, he suggested, they might bring about reform; instead he feared that lack of education and habitual 'subserviences' made them 'consenting parties to the miserable imbecility into which we have fallen'.

These feelings of despair and disillusion spilled over into his personal life. The children were growing up rapidly, and, much as he loved his large family, Dickens was discovering that they were by no means as tractable, and a good deal noisier, than the characters of his imagination. ('Why is it that a boy of that age should seem to have on at all times, 150 pairs of double soled boots and to be always jumping a bottom stair with the whole 150' he complained wryly of fourteen-year-old Walter.) When they were little he was full of ingenious ideas for plays and outings, dreaming

Following page:

'I have had all my children at home for the holidays,' Dickens wrote to his old friend Leigh Hunt, on 31 January 1855. He continues: 'My eldest boy … has required a good deal of my attention, … For my second boy … I have had to find a new probationary tutor. He has only this very day departed from the parental roof, with a plum cake, a box of marmalade, a ditto of jam, twelve oranges, five shillings, and a gross of tears!'

The British Library, Ashley MS. 637, f.1v

useful educational Institutions for the people in large towns. Redeeming autumn promises, I have been, since we met, in Berkshire, Dorsetshire, and Yorkshire. In the intervals and snatches of these expeditions, I have had all my children at home for the holidays - had been to Pantomimes - and had got up our annual Twelfth Night play at home, in which we all "go on" down to the Baby. My eldest boy, new-come home from Germany, has required a good deal of my attention, as he has to be armed against the Demon Idleness and started in busy life. For my second boy, destined for India, I have had to find a new probationary tutor. He has only this very day departed from the parental roof, with a Plum cake, a box of marmalade, a ditto of jam, twelve oranges, five shillings, and a

up elaborate nicknames for them and proudly regaling his friends with tales of their exploits; but as they grew older he expected them to conform to his high standards of punctuality and neatness, and to show something of his own energy and determination. Inevitably the boys suffered most under this exacting scrutiny, especially the eldest, Charley, a sensitive, unassertive boy who had been educated at Eton at Miss Coutts's expense. Not gifted academically, he had been allowed to leave school when he was fifteen to spend some time in Germany with the idea of going into business. Now aged seventeen, he returned from Leipzig not really sure of what he wanted to do: 'I think he has less fixed purpose and energy than I could have supposed possible in my son,' Dickens told Miss Coutts. 'He is not aspiring, or imaginative in his own behalf. With all the tenderer and better qualities which he inherits from his mother, he inherits an indescribable lassitude of character – a very serious thing in a man – which seems to me to express the want of a strong compelling hand always beside him.'

Angry, disappointed in his children and with a dawning realisation that he was no longer happy in his marriage, Dickens had little peace of mind during these years. His troubled mood was emphasised early in 1855 by two events which re-awakened powerful memories of the past. The first was the discovery that Gad's Hill Place, the house he had dreamed of owning as a child, was for sale: overcome by nostalgia, he could not resist making enquiries. Then, just a few days later, he received a letter from his first love, Maria Beadnell, now Mrs Winter. Although they had not entirely lost touch (he remained in occasional contact with her father), the sight of her handwriting at this sensitive time aroused unexpectedly intense emotions. He replied eagerly, recalling all his former passion, and for a few short weeks they exchanged intimate, sentimental reminiscences of their youth. But when they met he found that the enchanting girl he remembered was now fat and silly, with a coquettish manner ridiculous in a mature woman. The spell was broken, but the following year she appeared again – as the foolish Flora Finching in *Little Dorrit*.

The romance may have 'glided visibly away', as Forster suggested, but Dickens's reaction was symptomatic of his restless confusion at this time. 'It is much better to go on and fret, than to stop and fret. As to repose – for some men there's no such thing in this life … The old days! Shall I ever, I wonder, get the frame of mind back as it used to be then?' During the next two years he travelled frenetically between England and France, finding temporary respite in Paris during the winter of 1855–56, where he was delighted to

The engraved title page for the Library Edition of Little Dorrit *(1859), with a vignette after a painting by William Powell Frith.*

The British Library, 12603.k.9

discover that he was greeted everywhere as '*l'écrivain célèbre*' – the celebrated writer. Compared to glittering, sophisticated Paris, London was now a dark, 'vile place', and he began to wonder why he lived there. The English were insular, conservative and snobbish, and a visit to the English galleries at the Paris Universal Exhibition in November 1855 convinced him that even the artistic life of the country was being undermined. There was a 'horrid respectability' about most of the paintings, he noticed, 'a little, finite, systematic routine in them, strangely expressive to me of the state of England herself'.

Little Dorrit, the novel he was writing at this time, reflects all the sombre desolation of his mood. Originally entitled 'Nobody's Fault', it began as a relentless satire on the corrupt and apathetic state of contemporary society, but, as he became more interested in his characters, gradually developed into a complex study of individual helplessness and misery in a confused and oppressive world. Prisons are a powerful symbol throughout the book, in which many of the characters are trapped in actual or psychological situations as inescapable as the forbidding, high walls of the Marshalsea, home for over twenty years to the weak and selfish William Dorrit. Only his youngest daughter, Amy (Little Dorrit), finds freedom and, despite the overwhelming melancholy of the novel, her loving kindness eventually brings a measure of personal happiness to the middle-aged, despairing Arthur Clennam. Although Dickens boasted that he had never had so many readers, providing him with the largest payment of his career so far at over £11,000, the novel was harshly attacked by the critics. For many it confirmed the impression, left by *Bleak House*, that his creative powers were in decline, while others reacted furiously to his opportunist and subversive attacks on British institutions and government. It was pronounced 'decidedly the worst' of his novels, and at least one critic expressed serious doubt as to whether his books would last.

The Marshalsea had been closed during the 1840s and some of the buildings converted or demolished, but three days before he finished the novel he went to see what remained of the place he remembered so vividly from his childhood. The courtyard was gone, and so were the high walls, but the main prison block was still standing with 'the rooms that have been in my mind's eye in the story' – the rooms which had housed his father so long ago. For a while he stood silently 'among the crowding ghosts of many miserable years'.

The End of His Marriage 1857–58

Dickens was rapidly approaching a crisis in his life when his vague sense of 'something wanting', his irritation with Catherine, his impatience and claustrophobia, would finally become unendurable. Throughout the autumn of 1856 he tried to suppress his unhappiness in preparations for a production of Wilkie Collins's play, *The Frozen Deep*, to be performed during the coming Twelfth Night season. The Tavistock House schoolroom was elaborately converted for the occasion, and the cast, which included Mamie and Kate, Georgina and her younger sister Helen Hogarth, was subjected to gruelling rehearsals for weeks beforehand.

It was a melodramatic story inspired by recent controversial reports about Sir John Franklin's ill-fated Arctic expedition of 1845, but the main attraction for Dickens lay in the central character of Richard Wardour, the distraught and angry rejected lover. He threw all his restless energy into the part, transforming Collins's conventional villain into a tragic hero who, in a final scene of appalling misery, sacrifices himself to save the life of his rival. By the time the lights dimmed for the last time the audience was sobbing audibly, while Dickens himself was so overcome that for ten minutes he could only lie motionless on the stage. The reviews were wildly enthusiastic and for three weeks his acting was the talk of all London. He was exhilarated by the reaction, claiming that he had never seen people 'so strongly affected by theatrical means', but the raw emotion of his performance shocked his friends and family, and lived on in his imagination long after the play had been forgotten.

In February 1857 Dickens at last took possession of Gad's Hill, and, after a flurry of decorating and apparently endless excavations in search of a reliable water supply, a house-warming party was held in the garden on Catherine's birthday, 19 May. The plain 'little old-fashioned house' – situated, as he loved to tell his friends, on the very spot 'where Falstaff ran away' – obviously delighted him, even though he had no immediate plans to live there. For Hans Christian Andersen, visiting that summer, it was a magical place: '… there is a fragrance of clover, the elder tree is in blossom and the wild roses have an odour of apples …'. At the time he did not notice any tension between his host and hostess, but many years later he recalled that he had occasionally seen Catherine coming out of her room with tears in her eyes.

Gad's Hill offered Dickens peace and tranquillity, but he was unable to relax or find comfort at home. Early in June he was shocked to hear that his friend Douglas Jerrold had died unexpectedly. Without stopping to think that his actions would cause offence to the family, he immediately set about organising a benefit programme of lectures, readings and concerts, including a revival of *The Frozen Deep*. After a highly successful season at the Gallery of Illustration in London's Regent Street, which opened with a private performance for the Queen and her guests on 4 July, the play was taken to the new Free Trade Hall in Manchester. For this much larger venue professional actresses were engaged for the female parts, amongst them Mrs Frances Ternan, and her two younger daughters Maria and Ellen. Eighteen-year-old Nelly, 'small, fair-haired, rather pretty', played only a minor role, but Dickens was immediately fascinated by her charming manner and air of youthful innocence; according to his daughter, Kate, she came 'like a breath of spring' into his hard-working life 'and enslaved him'.

Dickens returned from Manchester in a state of anxious confusion and misery. 'My blankness is inconceivable – indescribable,' he told Collins; 'low spirits, low pulse, low voice, intense reaction.' It was not unusual for him to feel depressed and 'let down' at the end of a play, but this time, he told another friend, there seemed no way 'out of the dark corner'. To Forster he at last confided feelings which, until now, he had scarcely acknowledged even to himself: 'Poor Catherine and I are not made for each other, and there is no help for it. It is not only that she makes me uneasy and unhappy, but that I make her so too – and much more so.' He admitted that his difficult temperament and unsettled way of life were partly to blame, but it was too late for change: 'only one thing will alter that, and that is, the end which alters everything'.

In a desperate attempt to 'escape from myself', he persuaded Collins to join him on a walking tour of the Lake District with the aim of gathering material for a contribution to *Household Words*, but knowing that they would not be too far from Doncaster, where the Ternans were playing in their next engagement. 'The Lazy

Catherine Dickens, photographed by J. J. E. Mayall in 1852, the year she gave birth to her tenth and last child, Plorn. Mayall took several photographs of both Dickens and Catherine at about this time.

Charles Dickens Museum, London

Tour of Two Idle Apprentices', as described in the magazine, was no such thing, and even by Dickens's standards it was a 'wild', hopeless adventure, which did nothing to reconcile him to his situation. Shortly afterwards he took the irrevocable step of arranging for his dressing room at Tavistock House to be converted into a bedroom and the doorway leading to Catherine's room to be closed up with a set of shelves. To Forster's remonstrances he replied only 'Too late to say, put the curb on, and don't rush at hills. I have now no relief but in action.' Faced with Catherine's tears and recriminations he reacted angrily, just as he had ten years earlier in Genoa, confiding to Monsieur de la Rue: 'I don't get on better in these later times with a certain poor lady you know of, than I did in the earlier Peschiere days. Much worse … Neither can she get on with herself , or be anything but unhappy.' For once there were no celebrations at Christmas, and the boys stayed at school over the holidays, but Dickens told friends that he dreamed of ogres and rescuing his princess from dragon-guarded castles.

In this state of mind he could not settle down to writing, but his old idea for a series of readings from his books seemed to offer a way of keeping in touch with his public. Since his first performance at Birmingham in 1853 he had given several readings for charity, provoking such outpourings of tears and laughter in his listeners that it now struck him he might use his talent for his own benefit. Forster strongly opposed the suggestion, seeing it as a dangerous and degrading distraction from the serious business of authorship, and one which was only likely to upset and weary him still further; but Miss Coutts, who had never approved of his theatrical performances, surprisingly raised no objections – 'I think upon the whole, that most people would be glad you should have the money,' she agreed. Dickens needed no more encouragement: 'I must do *something*, or I shall wear my heart away,' he told Forster. He gave his first professional reading on 29 April at St Martin's Hall, walking stiffly onto the platform to a 'roar of cheering' from the large audience. By the end of the evening people were having to be turned away at the door, and it was decided to extend the original scheme for three performances to sixteen. With a tour of provincial towns already planned for the autumn, he was on the threshold of a second, highly successful and lucrative career which eventually led to almost 500 public performances.

For this first London season Dickens had chosen to read from the Christmas books, but even while he was conjuring up scenes of family harmony and benevolence for his listeners his own 'dismal failure' of a marriage, as it now seemed to him, was rapidly coming to an end. Within a month of his first professional appearance he and Catherine had agreed to a formal separation on terms which provided her with a small house of her own and an allowance of £600 a year. Charley chose to live with his mother, but the other children stayed with their father; so, too, did Georgina, much to the disapproval of the rest of the Hogarth family, and the amazement of London society as news of the troubles in the Dickens household began to spread. Rumours and lies led to yet more scurrilous rumours – some of which seem to have originated with Mrs Hogarth and her youngest daughter, Helen – that he was having an affair with an actress, or worse still, with his sister-in-law; there was even some talk, at least within the family, that Catherine might have grounds for divorce under the new Matrimonial Causes Act of 1857. Thackeray, who knew the Ternans, tried to correct the more damaging stories but succeeded only in provoking a serious quarrel with Dickens which they never fully resolved.

As the scandalous gossip threatened to spiral out of control Dickens fired off letters to his friends, fiercely protesting his innocence and asserting that there was 'no other cause' for his separation from Catherine than 'our having lived unhappily together for some time'. Filled with self-righteous indignation, he forced the Hogarths to sign a statement retracting their allegations, and, so that there could not be any further doubt, prepared his own personal declaration for publication in the press, solemnly denying the 'false' and 'monstrous' misrepresentations 'involving, not only me, but innocent persons dear to my heart'. Ignoring the horrified protests of his friends, he proceeded to publish this statement in *Household Words* and a number of other national and provincial papers, but among those which refused to carry it was *Punch*, edited by Mark Lemon and published by Bradbury and Evans. Although they had been close friends and colleagues for many years, Dickens took this as a personal insult. He cut himself off from Lemon, who remained a kindly supporter of Catherine, and immediately determined to sever all relations with his publishers, even though this led to a bitter dispute which had to be settled in the courts. Within a few months he had replaced *Household Words* with a new journal, *All the Year Round*, and begun the process of transferring all his copyrights back to Chapman and Hall.

Not content with publishing this extraordinary declaration, Dickens allowed himself to be goaded into preparing a much more explicit statement which he authorized Arthur Smith, manager of his readings, to circulate to anyone who still doubted his integrity. In this version – which he would later refer to as the 'violated letter' when it inevitably found its way into the newspapers – he heaped all the blame for the breakdown of their marriage onto Catherine. Claiming that she suffered from a 'mental disorder' which led to her 'increasing estrangement', he cruelly and falsely accused her of abandoning all care and responsibility for the children. Georgina, who had sacrificed the best part of her life to be their 'playmate, nurse, instructress, friend', he asserted, was the only effective mother they had ever known, and had it not been for her the marriage would have ended long ago. The papers were not convinced, and neither were his friends: 'He is $\frac{1}{2}$ mad about his domestic affairs, and tother $\frac{1}{2}$ mad with arrogance and vanity,' wrote Thackeray to his daughters.

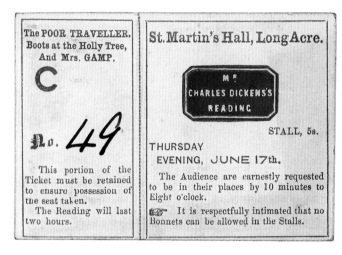

A ticket for a reading given during Dickens's first London season. The programme consisted of two of his Christmas stories followed by episodes from Martin Chuzzlewit.

The British Library, Dex. 316

Years afterwards, Kate acknowledged that 'this affair brought out all that was worst – all that was weakest in him. He did not care a damn what happened to any of us. Nothing could surpass the misery and unhappiness of our home.'

After her initial protests Catherine made no further attempt to defend herself. For the next twenty years she lived quietly at 70 Gloucester Crescent near Regent's Park, until her death from cancer in November 1879. She kept in touch with the children (except Mamie, who adored her father) and continued to see sympathetic friends such as Maclise, Collins and Miss Coutts. She did not meet Dickens again, and he tried to erase all memory of her from his mind, but she never ceased to care for him, nor to follow his career and read his books. Her faded copy of *The Uncommercial Traveller*, containing some of his last journalistic pieces, is now with the Dexter Collection of Dickens's manuscripts and books in The British Library; and

Tabistock House,
Tabistock Square. London. W.C.

Friday Fourth June 1858

Dear Catherine.

I will not write a word as to any *causes* that have made it necessary for me to publish the enclosed in Household Words. Whoever there may be among the living, whom I will never forgive alive or dead, I earnestly hope that all unkindness is over between You and me.

But as you are referred to in the article, I think you ought to see it. You have only to say to Wills (who kindly brings it to you), that you do not object to the allusion.

Charles Dickens

Dickens's twenty-two-year marriage to Catherine ended bitterly in June 1858. This letter, enclosing a copy of the personal statement he was about to publish in Household Words, was one of the last he wrote to her.

The British Library,
Add. MS 43689, f.288

she was present at the first night of a dramatization of *Dombey and Son* in 1873, unable to hold back her tears. His letters remained amongst her most treasured possessions until one afternoon, towards the end of her life, she entrusted them to her daughter, Kate, with earnest instructions that they, too, should be given to the Library 'so that the world may know he loved me once'.

As time passed Kate regretted that she had not been more supportive of her 'sweet, kind' mother who bore these lonely years with such dignity. Catherine was not lively or particularly intelligent, she did not shine in company and was no match for her husband's restless brilliance. Yet, as Henry Morley observed when he met her in 1851: 'One sees in five minutes that she loves her husband and her children, and has a warm heart for anybody who won't be satirical, but meet her on her own good-natured footing.' In later years Dickens dismissed his marriage as a 'miserable mistake' made when he was very young, but, looking back over her parents' lives in 1906, Kate wrote to G. K. Chesterton: 'I feel sure that at the time she became engaged to my father, [my mother] was a very winning and affectionate creature, and although the marriage turned out a "dismal failure" … I am also convinced that my dear father gained much from her refining influence.' 'I fancy,' she continued, 'they had several years of very great happiness before my poor father found out his "mistake" and before my poor mother suffered from his discovery. They were both to be pitied.'

Dickens had behaved very badly and, after all that had happened, he might have wanted to rest at home away from intrusive scrutiny and criticism. Instead, he put his faith in his public, which – in spite of everything – remained unfailingly loyal and enthusiastic. During 1858 he made more speeches than ever before, including one of his most memorable appeals on behalf of the Hospital for Sick Children in Great Ormond Street; he launched the Library Edition of his works, elegantly designed to appeal to wealthier readers; and his first reading tour, which took him to forty-three towns as far apart as Brighton, Glasgow and Limerick, was a triumph. One friend who had not seen him for many years thought he was greatly changed – his hair grizzled and thinning, his lined face partly concealed by the beard and moustache he had grown for *The Frozen Deep*, his once frank and open expression now care-worn and clouded. But he still dressed with the same meticulous care, wearing a large gold watch-chain across his chest and a flower in his buttonhole for his readings, walking as always with the 'military precision' Henry James observed so perceptively, his head held high and his expressive eyes as bright and piercing as ever.

Opposite page:

Dickens posed as if to give a reading, photographed by Herbert Watkins in 1859.

The British Library, Dex. 316

❧ *Celebrated Author 1859–65*

Ellen Ternan changed Dickens's life. Outwardly he remained one of the most celebrated of all Victorians, the greatest writer of his day, an outspoken defender of the poor and the oppressed, and an irresistible entertainer forever associated with domestic warmth and happiness. Privately he was an increasingly remote figure, cut off from many of his old friends, spending as much time as possible with Nelly (as he liked to call her), who now lived in retirement with her mother and sisters in a house he leased for her in Houghton Place, a short walk from Tavistock House. Even today very little is known about their relationship. At the time of his separation Dickens insisted that it was purely platonic, and although recent biographical research (including a careful reading of some of his later stories), together with occasional references to a child who died, strongly suggests that they eventually became lovers, there is still no firm evidence to support this assumption. None of their correspondence survives, and she is mentioned only fleetingly in a

An advertisement for Dickens's new periodical All the Year Round, *featuring* A Tale of Two Cities. *Much of the magazine's success was due to an extensive publicity campaign which saw thousands of handbills and posters circulated throughout the country.*

The British Library,
Dex. 316

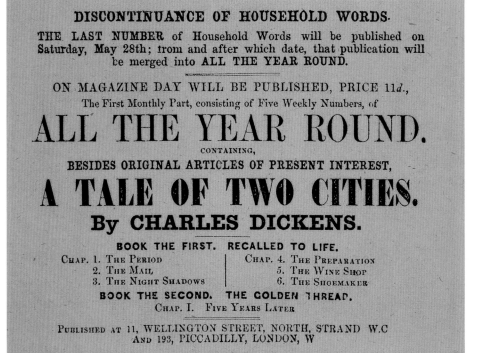

DISCONTINUANCE OF HOUSEHOLD WORDS.

THE LAST NUMBER of Household Words will be published on Saturday, May 28th; from and after which date, that publication will be merged into ALL THE YEAR ROUND.

ON MAGAZINE DAY WILL BE PUBLISHED, PRICE 11*d*.,

The First Monthly Part, consisting of Five Weekly Numbers, of

ALL THE YEAR ROUND.

CONTAINING,

BESIDES ORIGINAL ARTICLES OF PRESENT INTEREST,

A TALE OF TWO CITIES.

By CHARLES DICKENS.

BOOK THE FIRST. RECALLED TO LIFE.

Chap. 1. The Period	Chap. 4. The Preparation
2. The Mail	5. The Wine Shop
3. The Night Shadows	6. The Shoemaker

BOOK THE SECOND. THE GOLDEN THREAD.

Chap. I. Five Years Later

Published at 11, WELLINGTON STREET, NORTH, STRAND W.C
And 193, PICCADILLY, LONDON, W

handful of letters to the very few friends who knew about her – just often enough to show that his life revolved around her, his feelings, if anything, growing deeper and more poignant as the years went by.

There is a glimpse of her in the loving description of Lucie Manette, the heroine of *A Tale of Two Cities*, the historical romance he wrote to launch *All the Year Round* in April 1859. The novel – a powerful expression of all the passionate emotions which had been in his mind since he played the part of Richard Wardour, set against the horrific backdrop of the French Revolution – was enthusiastically received by the public. By June 1859 Dickens was able to report that *All the Year Round* was an 'amazing success', far outselling *Household Words* with an average circulation of 100,000, rising to 300,000 for the Christmas numbers. At a time of rapid expansion and competition in the periodical press, it became known for the high quality of the fiction: *A Tale of Two Cities* was followed by Wilkie Collins's *The Woman in White*, Mrs Gaskell's *A Dark Night's Work*, Bulwer Lytton's *A Strange Story* and, in the years to come, three of Trollope's last works, *Is He Popenjoy?*, *The Duke's Children* and *Mr Scarborough's Family*.

Professionally, 1859 was a rewarding year for Dickens, especially after the turmoil of the recent past. Yet the breakdown of his marriage had left him to bear his family responsibilities alone, and there were times, he confided to Wills, when he felt 'quite weighed down and loaded and chained ... by the enormous drags upon me'. First his father, then his brothers had proved incapable of managing their lives; now he was afraid that the pattern might be repeated in his sons. His letters written during the years immediately following his separation from Catherine show that he

Ellen Ternan, photographed in 1858 or 1859, within a year or two of her first meeting with Dickens.

Charles Dickens Museum, London

worried constantly about their apparent lack of direction and talent as, one by one, they failed to meet his expectations and were encouraged to pursue careers far from home. Charley, the eldest, still struggling to make his way in business, greatly distressed his father by marrying Bessie Evans, the daughter of his former publisher; only the birth of a first grandchild in 1862 helped to heal the breach. Walter, who had joined the Indian army with high hopes in 1857, was already accumulating large debts. Frank, an anxious boy with a pronounced stammer, seemed to be in a 'desultory, unprofitable kind of state', his father thought, during 1860 and had to be found work in the *All the Year Round* office before he, too, left for India. Alfred, 'a good steady fellow but not at all brilliant', failed to obtain the army commission he had hoped for and eventually emigrated to Australia in 1865. Thirteen-year-old Sydney, with his heart set on becoming a sailor, joined the navy as a midshipman. Of the two youngest boys, Henry, aged eleven in 1860, was already showing signs of the ability which would lead him – alone of all Dickens's sons – to university and a successful career in the law; whereas Plorn, a shy, diffident child, was doomed, like most of his brothers, to an unsettled and unsatisfactory life overseas.

Even his daughters, now in their early twenties, were giving cause for anxiety. Although Dickens wrote cheerfully about the new arrangements at home – 'My eldest daughter is a capital housekeeper, heads the table gracefully, delegates certain appointed duties to her sister and aunt, and they are all three devotedly attached ...' – they were treated coolly by some of the more censorious sections of London society. Mamie, who never married, was clearly out of sorts during this period, spending much of her time away visiting friends. Kate, always her father's favourite and the most like him in temperament, decided to marry Wilkie Collins's sickly brother, Charles, simply, it was said, to escape from 'an unhappy home'. The wedding, which took place on 17 July 1860, was an uncomfortable affair: many of the guests, knowing that Dickens strongly disapproved, were uncertain how to behave, and Catherine's absence could not fail to be noticed.

With his family gradually moving out into the world, Dickens no longer needed a large house in London. Tavistock House was filled with too many unhappy memories and he now decided to spend most of each year at Gad's Hill, renting a furnished house in town for the winter season and using a small flat over the

Standing, from right to left, on the steps of the front porch at Gad's Hill are Dickens with his daughters Mamie and Katey, and his friend Henry Chorley. Seated are Katey's husband Charles Collins and Georgina. This photograph of Dickens, one of several taken by Robert Hindry Mason in August 1866, was considered an exceptionally good likeness.

The British Library, Dex. 316

All the Year Round office for occasional visits. Many of the fixtures and fittings he had carefully chosen only nine years earlier were sold with the house, but in the field behind Gad's Hill he ruthlessly burned basket after basket of letters and papers, while Harry and Plorn, as they still remembered many years afterwards, 'roasted onions in the ashes of the great'. From this time onwards he made a point of destroying all his personal letters as soon as he had read them, and – bearing in mind the prying eyes of potential biographers – of keeping his own as short as possible.

During this difficult period of readjustment Dickens began to write a series of quietly reflective, often hauntingly beautiful, essays for *All the Year Round*. Adopting the persona of the 'Uncommercial Traveller', he recorded his impressions of places and people he met on his solitary walks through the streets of London or journeys through the countryside. He described soup kitchens, railway waiting rooms, workhouses, prisons, and the back streets and by-ways of shabby city neighbourhoods. He revisited the melancholy Inns of Court, deserted churches and cheap theatres, scenes of some of his youthful *Sketches*; and he returned to the Rochester of his childhood, reliving with almost painful intensity the innocent pleasures and night-time fears which had shaped his imagination so many years ago. Like Jarvis Lorry in *A Tale of Two Cities*, he was beginning to find comfort in such memories: 'My heart is touched now, by many remembrances that had long fallen asleep, ... by many associations of the days when what we call the World was not so real with me, and my faults were not confirmed in me.'

Great Expectations, he told Forster, began as one of his 'Uncommercial Traveller' essays, but developed into such a 'very fine, new and grotesque idea' that he decided to reserve it for his next book. It traces, with great delicacy and understanding, the story of Pip, a confused and frightened child who is deluded by the prospect of an unexpected fortune into disowning his humble friends and origins, until, through a humiliating journey of self-discovery, he learns the bitter truth about his 'great expectations'. Written, like *David Copperfield*, in the first person, it is a penetrating re-examination of Dickens's own inner life – of the regrets and disappointments which were particularly in his mind at this time, and which speak to everyone who has set out on life with high hopes and ambitions. At the end of the novel as originally written, Pip and Estella part, leaving Pip a lonely yet wiser man;

Great Expectations *was not illustrated when it first appeared in Britain. This plate by John McLenan is from an early American edition published by T. B. Peterson in Philadelphia.*

The British Library, Cup.400.b.17

but Bulwer Lytton persuaded him to substitute a gentler conclusion, suggesting that they eventually find happiness together. 'Upon the whole I think it is for the better,' Dickens acknowledged.

Immediately acclaimed as a masterpiece, *Great Expectations* was a success on both sides of the Atlantic. In Britain it was issued in three volumes soon after its completion in *All the Year Round* – an unusual form of publication for Dickens, but one which was popular with circulating library readers; in America its serialization in *Harper's Weekly* was followed by a string of editions in book form, several with illustrations by American artists. During the 1860s Dickens's audience expanded rapidly at home and abroad as he and his publishers brought out new editions of his works to suit all levels of the market:

the People's Edition (designed for railway bookstalls) and the Charles Dickens Edition (slightly revised and containing new prefaces by the author) were extensively advertised and promoted throughout the English-speaking world. In Europe his works were widely available as part of Tauchnitz's Series of English Writers, as well as in translation – indeed in France, he proudly observed, translations could be found at every station. He could now routinely command £1,000 for a short story for an American magazine, and invitations for readings came from as far away as Australia.

Yet Dickens found happiness elusive. Throughout this period he travelled 'perpetually' to France, often using deliberately evasive language about his visits. Many were spent in the quiet village of Condette, six miles south of Boulogne, at a modest farmhouse belonging to his old friend M. Beaucourt-Mutuel, and although there is no certainty that Nelly stayed there, it seems likely that she and her mother were living nearby. His letters point to a turning point in their relationship at the height of these visits during 1862 and 1863 – perhaps her pregnancy, and the baby's subsequent death – which left him tortured by uncertainty, distress and 'miserable anxieties'. He was also concerned about Georgina, usually so dependable but suffering from low spirits and a heart condition throughout much of 1862: 'No one can ever know what she has been to us,' he told Macready, 'and how she has supplied an empty place and an ever-widening gap since the girls were mere dolls.' These were years which saw the deaths of Arthur Smith, manager of his reading tours; of Augustus Egg, Thackeray, and John Leech; of his mother, his brother Alfred, and his son Walter, who died in India at the age of twenty-three. 'It is easy to say that in this hard life we must close up the ranks, whosoever falls, and march on ...' he wrote, 'but my heart faints sometimes under such troubles as I do know, and if it were not for a certain stand-up determination, I should lie down.'

Many times during this period he thought of starting a new book in monthly parts, but it was not until January 1864 that he was able to report that he had written the opening number, and even then, he admitted, he felt 'dazed' by the return to the 'large canvas' and 'big brushes'. First published between May 1864 and November 1865, *Our Mutual Friend* was Dickens's last completed novel and, in some ways, a culmination of all his earlier work. The London he describes is now a rapidly expanding city, a 'gritty' chaos of unfinished streets and black ditches, of dust-heaps

Following pages:

A view of the river Thames by Thomas Shotter Boys, from London As It Is *(1842), showing Blackfriars' Bridge. Although crowded and increasingly polluted, the 'black highway', as Dickens described it in one of his essays, dominated London's commercial life.*

Guildhall Library

103

and the silent, polluting river. It is a hollow world, dominated by greed and self-interest, and the superficial, deeply destructive values of the new middle classes; a world of death and deception where money corrupts even the poor as they struggle for survival at the margins of society. It is ruthless, joyless, and very different from the boisterous old England of *Pickwick Papers* – a change emphasised by Dickens's decision to replace Browne with a new young artist, Marcus Stone, whose realistic illustrations gave a much more contemporary 'feel' to the novel.

On 9 June 1865, with *Our Mutual Friend* almost completed, Dickens was returning from a brief holiday in France with Ellen and her mother when the train in which they were travelling was involved in a serious accident, near Staplehurst in Kent. Several carriages plunged from the track, killing ten passengers and injuring many more. Nelly was slightly hurt by the impact – in subsequent letters she is often described as 'the Patient' – but Dickens managed to lead his two companions to safety before returning to the terrible scene to help with the rescue operation. Throughout the hot afternoon he tirelessly administered water and brandy from his flask as he tried to comfort the wounded and dying. It was only later that he thought to retrieve his manuscript from the wreckage, remembering 'with devout thankfulness', as he wrote in a postscript to the novel, 'that I can never be much nearer parting company with my readers for ever than I was then, until there shall be written against my life the two words with which I have this day closed this book: THE END'

Opposite page:

St Mary Overy's Dock, photographed in 1886 by the Society for Photographing Relics of Old London. Our Mutual Friend *opens in London's docklands, an area Dickens knew well from his visits to his godfather as a boy.*

The British Library, Tab.700.b.3

〜 *Final Years 1865–70*

Dickens was profoundly shaken by the accident and by the painful scenes he had witnessed. Long afterwards he complained of feeling sick and weak, and generally 'not quite right within'; he became conscious of an alteration in his pulse which his doctor attributed to a weakness of the heart; and the gout he had already begun to suffer from gradually worsened, so that for the rest of his life he was troubled by attacks of crippling pain when he could scarcely bear even a slipper on his left foot. Most debilitating of all were the psychological scars which left him with a 'nervous dread' of railway travel: there were no more mysterious visits to France and whenever possible he avoided express trains, even though this seriously added to the stress and discomfort of his reading tours.

Increasingly, Dickens looked for rest and comfort at Gad's Hill, which he had now transformed into an elegant and well-appointed home. He built a new drawing-room, added a conservatory, commissioned specially designed parquet floors for the hall and landing, and converted the old coach-house into a splendid servants' hall. The gardens were laid out with neat lawns, flower beds filled with his favourite scarlet geraniums, and a shrubbery where he erected the chalet given to him by the French actor Charles Fechter, which made a magical, secluded writing room in summer. Here at his 'little country house' he was very much a local celebrity, not often socialising with his neighbours, but a familiar figure as he strode along the lanes with his dogs loping at his heels, or handed out prizes at sports days or cricket matches in the field behind the house. As time went by he introduced Nelly to Georgina and his daughters, and she became an occasional visitor to Gad's Hill or a discreet presence at some of his readings. But for the most part she remained hidden in the background, living quietly in Slough or Peckham, in houses he rented for her under the name of Charles Tringham, a pseudonym he may have taken from the name of his tobacconist near the *All the Year Round* office.

In 1866, although he was far from well, Dickens accepted a proposal from the impresarios Chappell and Co. for a provincial reading tour at a fee of £50 a night. The arrangements went smoothly, he enjoyed the return to the stage after an absence

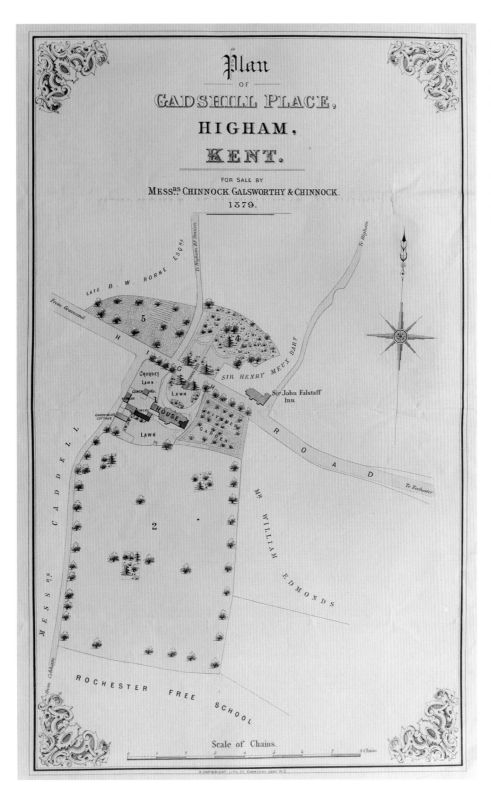

of three years and his audiences were as appreciative as ever. It was inevitable that he should begin to feel inexorably 'drawn towards America', where he had many friends and an eager, admiring public. His motive was largely financial: he had his wife's allowance to pay, his own expensive position to maintain, Nelly to support, and sons who continued to give cause for anxiety. He was well aware that it would be a demanding undertaking but, as he explained to Wills, at the age of fifty-five the prospect of making a large sum of money very quickly was 'an immense consideration'. The main obstacle was his reluctance to be parted from his 'dearest girl', and although he sent frequent letters and messages via Wills, who acted as go-between, he clearly missed her dreadfully during the six months he was away.

He arrived in Boston on 19 November 1867 to find that people had been queueing for up to twelve hours in the freezing cold for tickets, and the first four readings were already sold out. Contrary to expectations, there was no immediate revival of the hostilities which had marred his previous visit, nor – despite the crowds which rushed to greet him – of the intrusive behaviour he had so resented in 1842. Boston was now a large mercantile city, and New York, where everything looked as if it 'grew newer every day, instead of older', had changed out of all recognition. The cost of living, he noticed immediately, was 'enormous', but this time he could afford to stay in the best hotels where his meals were served in his own rooms and he was assured of peace and privacy. He resolutely avoided public dinners and functions, preferring to concentrate on his readings, but he enjoyed meeting old friends such as Longfellow (now 'perfectly white in hair and beard'), and the publisher James Fields, who with his charming wife, Annie, opened their home to him.

'Au Revoir!' Dickens, surrounded by his characters, says farewell to John Bull as he leaves for America. Cartoon by John Proctor, published in Judy, *30 October 1867.*

The British Library, Dex. 316

The readings in Boston, New York, Washington and Philadelphia were an enormous success, but despite the watchful care of George Dolby, his efficient new manager, Dickens's health and spirits deteriorated sharply as the tour progressed. He caught a cold which turned to influenza in the bitter winter weather; his voice was hoarse and he found it difficult to sleep; Christmas Day was spent on an 'intolerable' train journey from Boston to New York, and although he told Mamie that he 'plucked up a little' after a meal and some hot gin punch it was as much as he could do to read the following evening. Tentative plans to include Chicago and the West had to be given up, but this still left a gruelling programme of seventy-six performances with all the travelling and preparation that entailed. Remarkably, he seemed to draw strength from his audiences and was delighted by the spontaneous round of applause which greeted him on his birthday in February, but he was now so exhausted that he often collapsed as soon as the reading was over. By the end of the visit he was existing on a self-imposed regime of soup, beef tea, sherry and champagne, and in such intense pain that he had to be helped on to the platform for his final appearances. He completed the tour on 20 April, having made a profit of almost £20,000 – far more than expected – but the effort had affected him severely.

Dickens arrived home surprisingly restored by the voyage, but knowing that his next extended series of 100 readings would be his last. During the coming weeks he was preoccupied with *All the Year Round* and with a sad parting from his youngest son, Plorn, who left to join his brother, Alfred, in Australia, but as autumn approached he began to plan his final programme. Determined to leave his audiences with the memory of 'something very passionate and dramatic', he now prepared a deliberately horrifying adaptation of the murder scene from *Oliver Twist*. At first reluctant to unleash such powerful emotions in public, he soon became obsessed with the piece, performing it night after night even though it left him physically and emotionally exhausted. Throughout the spring of 1869 he stubbornly refused to acknowledge his failing health, but on 22 April, after suffering a stroke which left him feeling 'giddy, jarred, shaken, faint' and complaining of extreme weakness and loss of vision on his left side, he was forced to abandon the tour on the intructions of his doctors.

*The High Street
in Rochester, Kent,
c.1902. The city
features in many
of Dickens's novels
and stories, and
provided the model
for Dullborough Town
in* The Uncommercial
Traveller *essays and
Cloisterham in*
The Mystery of
Edwin Drood.

*The British Library,
10350.ee.9*

The final page of the manuscript of The Mystery of Edwin Drood, *written on 8 June 1870. It describes a 'brilliant' summer morning when 'changes of glorious light from moving boughs, songs of birds, scents from gardens, woods and fields ... penetrate into the Cathedral, subdue its earthy odour, and preach the Resurrection and the Life'.*

Victoria and Albert Museum

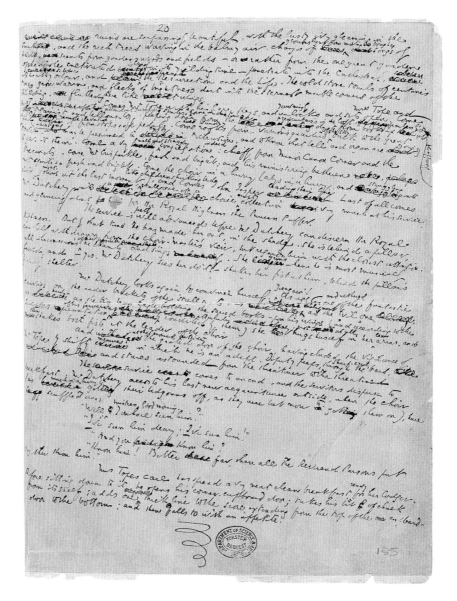

The summer was spent quietly in London and at Gad's Hill. He was soon assuring friends that he felt in 'brilliant condition', yet Dolby missed his 'old vivacity and elasticity of spirit' and Annie Fields noticed the sadness in his eyes when she and her husband visited him in London later that year. In May he made a new will, leaving the bulk of his estate to be divided equally between his children, but including, amongst a small number of individual bequests, £1000 to 'Miss Ellen Lawless Ternan, late of Houghton Place' – a strangely public statement of a relationship he had kept secret for so long. He appointed Charley sub-editor of

All the Year Round in place of Wills, who retired following a riding accident, and arranged for a new agreement formalising his arrangements with Chapman and Hall. He completed a third series of 'Uncommercial' essays, and then, in August, after an interval of four years, he started work on a new novel.

The Mystery of Edwin Drood was designed to be published in twelve instead of the usual twenty monthly numbers. As one of its earliest critics observed, it is strikingly different from his earlier work – more in tune with its times perhaps, shorter, tighter, and owing much to the recent vogue for 'sensation' novels, especially exotic mystery stories like *The Moonstone*, which had been such a triumph for Wilkie Collins in 1868. Instead of the biting social criticism of the later books, there is a carefully crafted atmosphere of secrecy and sinister decay in which the hushed walls of Cloisterham become the setting for an extraordinary study of hypnosis, opium addiction, uncontrollable passion and murder. Yet Dickens is always more than a good storyteller, and in this work he is also, as F. R. Leavis noticed, a 'great poet' evoking, in some of his most lyrical prose, his own final progress from Rochester, his first and last home, through death to resurrection.

'Sleeping it off.' Illustration by Samuel Luke Fildes (1844–1927) for the final number of The Mystery of Edwin Drood. *Dickens's son-in-law, Charles Collins, was to have illustrated the novel but illness prevented him from completing more than the cover design. The painter John Everett Millais suggested Fildes as a replacement. Fildes took great pains over his drawing, using real models and visiting an opium den in London's East End for accuracy.*

The British Library, Dex. 282

The Empty Chair,
Gad's Hill – Ninth of
June 1870 *by Samuel
Luke Fildes. This
watercolour, painted
shortly after Dickens's
death, uses the image
of the empty chair
featured in 'Sleeping
it off' but here there is
no candle to symbolise
life. Van Gogh was
deeply moved by this
image when he saw it
reproduced in the
Graphic later that
year: 'There is no
writer, in my opinion,'
he wrote, 'who is so
much a painter and a
black-and-white artist
as Dickens.'*

Free Library of Philadelphia

Dolby, who saw Dickens frequently during this time, said the writing gave him much 'trouble and anxiety'. Against medical advice, he insisted on giving twelve final readings at St James's Hall in London, beginning in the New Year. By now his doctor was in constant attendance, anxiously monitoring his pulse as it soared to 124, but many people who attended his last performance on 15 March 1870 thought he had never read so well. As his closing words died away, there was a brief hush and then, his son recalled, there was 'a storm of cheering as I have never seen equalled in my life'. These were Dickens's last weeks in London, and during this time he – who had never cared for Society, and had only recently reaffirmed his lack of political faith in 'the people who govern us' – was showered with invitations to meet members of the Establishment. He had a private audience with the Queen; attended a reception at Buckingham Palace; breakfasted with the Prime Minister; dined with Lord Stanhope, where he met Disraeli, and with Lord Houghton, where he was presented to the Prince of Wales. On 7 April he gave a lavish party for his friends – a charming host, as always, in spite of his pain; he spoke in public for the last time at the Royal Academy banquet on 30 April, when he replied to the toast to 'Literature'. There were rumours that he had been offered a title, but these appear to be unfounded and, in any case, he made no secret of his determination to remain simply Charles Dickens.

Tired at last of dining out at 'preposterous hours and preposterous places', he returned to Gad's Hill at the beginning of June, where Kate found him looking unusually grey and tired when she visited at the weekend. That Sunday evening they sat in the new conservatory, talking far into the night about her thoughts of going on the stage, about his life and his regrets that he had not been 'a better father – a better man'. He spoke of Ellen, and of his plans for *Edwin Drood*, 'if please God, I live to finish it'. The next morning he was up early as usual, anxious to complete his monthly number, but two days later, after working long into the afternoon, he suffered another severe stroke. He never regained consciousness and died, at the age of fifty-eight, on the following day, 9 June 1870, exactly five years after the fateful accident at Staplehurst. *The Mystery of Edwin Drood* remained unfinished.

Dickens had left explicit instructions in his will that he wished to be buried in an 'inexpensive, unostentatious and strictly private manner', with none of the 'revolting absurdity' usually associated with Victorian funerals. A grave was prepared in Rochester Cathedral, but in the days following his death it became clear that the nation wanted him to be buried in Westminster Abbey. Early on the morning of 14 June his body was taken by special train to London, where it was transferred to a plain hearse for the short journey from Charing Cross to the abbey. The service, read by the Dean, was attended only by his immediate family and a few close friends; in accordance with his request there was no address, and no hymns – just the organ playing softly as the simple oak coffin was lowered gently into the ground. Later that afternoon, however, crowds began to gather in the silent abbey and, as the news spread through the country and across the world, thousands of people from all walks of life arrived to pay tribute. Day after day they filed past, and for months to come his tombstone was covered with fresh flowers, as if, in Forster's words, 'a personal bereavement had befallen everyone'. Their remembrance, and the legacy of his work, were the only memorials Dickens ever wanted.

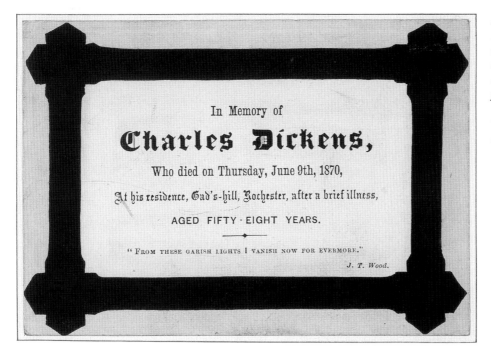

In Memory of

Charles Dickens,

Who died on Thursday, June 9th, 1870,

At his residence, Gad's-hill, Rochester, after a brief illness,

AGED FIFTY-EIGHT YEARS.

"FROM THESE GARISH LIGHTS I VANISH NOW FOR EVERMORE."

J. T. Wood.

A mourning card for Dickens, inscribed with the words he had spoken in farewell to his public after his final reading.

The British Library, Dex. 316

Charles Dickens

During his second visit to America in 1867–68 Dickens was photographed by Ben Gurney of Jeremiah Gurney and Son. This is one of several photographs taken during that session which were widely circulated to help publicize his tour. Dickens thought them among the best he had ever had taken.

The British Library, Dex.316

❧ *Chronology*

1812   Charles Dickens born on 7 February in Portsmouth.

1817   The family moves to Chatham where Charles attends William Giles's school.

1822   Dickens's father, John, recalled to London; the family settles at 16 Bayham Street, Camden Town.

1824   Dickens sent to work at Warren's Blacking Warehouse. His father is arrested for debt and imprisoned in the Marshalsea from March until 28 May.

1825   Dickens leaves the blacking factory and resumes his education at Wellington House Academy.

1827   Starts work as a solicitor's clerk.

1829   Having taught himself shorthand, Dickens becomes a reporter at Doctors' Commons.

1830   Falls in love with Maria Beadnell.

1831   Starts career as a journalist, reporting for *The Mirror of Parliament*.

1833   First publication, 'A Dinner at Poplar Walk', published in the December issue of *The Monthly Magazine*.

1834   Joins the staff of the *Morning Chronicle*.

1836   *Sketches by Boz*, first series, published on 8 February. The first monthly number of *Pickwick Papers* is published in March, and two days later, on 2 April, Dickens marries Catherine Hogarth. In December he leaves the *Morning Chronicle* to devote himself to his writing. During the winter he is introduced to Forster for the first time.

1837   First number of *Bentley's Miscellany*, edited by Dickens, appears on 1 January; *Oliver Twist* serialized in twenty-four instalments from the second number. First child, Charley, born on 6 January. In April Dickens and his family move to 48 Doughty Street; Mary Hogarth dies there on 7 May.

1838   Birth of second child, Mary, on 6 March. First number of *Nicholas Nickleby* published later that month.

1839   Resigns editorship of *Bentley's Miscellany*. *Nicholas Nickleby* published in book form in October, shortly before the birth of Dickens's second daughter, Kate. Family moves to 1 Devonshire Terrace. Dickens meets the heiress Angela Burdett Coutts.

1840   First issue of Dickens's weekly magazine, *Master Humphrey's Clock*, published on
        4 April; serialization of *The Old Curiosity Shop* begins on 25 April.

1841   *Barnaby Rudge* published in forty-two weekly numbers in *Master Humphrey's
        Clock* from 13 February. Birth of fourth child, Walter.

1842   In January Dickens and Catherine set out on a six-month visit to America. *American
        Notes* published in October; *Martin Chuzzlewit* begins serialization in twenty
        monthly parts in December.

1843   *A Christmas Carol* published 19 December.

1844   Birth of his fifth child, Francis. Dickens leaves Chapman and Hall; Bradbury and
        Evans become his publishers. In July takes his family, now including Catherine's
        sister Georgina, to Genoa. *The Chimes* published 16 December.

1845   Travels through Italy with his family before returning to London in July. In
        September directs and acts in a production of *Every Man in His Humour*.
        Birth of sixth child, Alfred, in October. *The Cricket on the Hearth* published
        20 December.

1846   Editor of the *Daily News* for a brief period in January and February. Publication of
        Pictures from Italy. Returns to the continent; serialization of *Dombey and Son* in
        twenty monthly parts begins in September. *The Battle of Life* published
        19 December.

1847   Returns from Paris; seventh child, Sydney, born. Heavily involved in helping to set
        up Urania Cottage, Miss Coutt's 'Home for Homeless Women'. Publication of
        the Cheap Edition of his works begins.

1848   On tour with the Amateur Players during the summer. Death of his much-loved
        sister, Fanny, in September. *The Haunted Man*, his last Christmas book,
        published in December.

1849   Birth of eighth child, Henry. Serialization of his favourite novel, *David Copperfield*,
        begins in April.

1850   First issue of *Household Words* published on 30 March. Birth of Dickens's ninth
        child, Dora.

1851   Deaths of Dickens's father, John, and the baby Dora. Directs and acts in Bulwer
        Lytton's play, *Not So Bad As We Seem*, to raise money for the Guild of
        Literature and Art. Family moves to Tavistock House.

1852   Monthly serialization of *Bleak House* begins in February. Birth of Edward, his
        tenth child.

1853   Family spends the summer in Boulogne. First public reading of *A Christmas Carol* in Birmingham.

1854   *Hard Times* serialized in *Household Words*.

1855   Meets Maria Beadnell again. In October Dickens takes his family to Paris for six months. First number of *Little Dorrit* published in December.

1856   Purchases Gad's Hill Place.

1857   Directs and acts in Collins's *The Frozen Deep*; meets Ellen Ternan who takes one of the female parts for public performances at Manchester.

1858   Gives his first paid public readings in London during the spring. In May he separates from Catherine, and publishes his personal statement in *Household Words*. First provincial reading tour, August–November.

1859   First issue of *All the Year Round* appears on 30 April, with the opening instalment of *A Tale of Two Cities*. Second provincial reading tour takes place during the autumn.

1860   First series of 'The Uncommercial Traveller' essays published in *All the Year Round*; serialization of *Great Expectations* begins in December.

1861   *Great Expectations* published in three volumes. Third provincial reading tour starts in October.

1862–63 Makes several visits to France. Death of his mother in September, and of his son Walter in December 1863.

1864   Serialization of *Our Mutual Friend* in twenty monthly parts begins in May.

1865   Dickens and Ellen involved in railway accident at Staplehurst on 9 June. *Our Mutual Friend* published in two volumes in November.

1866   Fourth reading tour in London and the provinces.

1867   In November arrives in Boston to begin American reading tour.

1868   Returns to England in April. In October, despite his poor health, begins a farewell reading tour.

1869   First public reading of 'Sikes and Nancy' on 5 January.

1870   Dickens received by Queen Victoria on 9 March. He gives his final reading on 15 March. First of six monthly numbers of *The Mystery of Edwin Drood* published in April. Dickens dies on 9 June following a severe stroke.

A musical tribute to Dickens, composed for Andrew Halliday's Little Em'ly *which opened at the Olympic Theatre in October 1869 – just one of the countless imitations, dramatizations, adaptations, souvenirs and memorabilia of all kinds inspired by his work.*

The British Library, h.1486.g(45)

❧ *Further Reading*

Original Works

Charles Dickens' Uncollected Writings from 'Household Words', edited by Harry Stone, 2 vols
(Allen Lane, 1969)

Dickens's Journalism, edited by Michael Slater, 4 vols (J. M. Dent, 1994–2000)

The Pilgrim Edition of the Letters of Charles Dickens, edited by Nina Burgis, Angus Easson,
Madeline House, Graham Storey, Kathleen Tillotson, K. J. Fielding, 12 vols
(Clarendon Press, 1965–2002)

The Speeches of Charles Dickens, edited by K. J. Fielding (Clarendon Press, 1960)

Biographies

Peter Ackroyd *Dickens* (Sinclair Stevenson, 1990)

Michael Allen *Charles Dickens' Childhood* (Macmillan, 1988)

John Forster *The Life of Charles Dickens*, 3 vols (Chapman & Hall, 1872–74)

Edgar Johnson *Charles Dickens: His Tragedy and Triumph* (Gollancz, 1953)

Fred Kaplan *Dickens: A Biography* (Hodder & Stoughton, 1988)

Claire Tomalin *The Invisible Woman: The Story of Nelly Ternan and Charles Dickens*
(Penguin, 1991)

Other Works

John Butt and Kathleen Tillotson *Dickens at Work* (Methuen, 1968)

John Carey *The Violent Effigy: A Study of Dickens's Imagination* (Faber & Faber, 1973)

G. K. Chesterton *Charles Dickens* (Methuen, 1906)

Philip Collins *Dickens: The Critical Heritage* (Routledge & Kegan Paul, 1971)

The Dickensian (Dickens Fellowship, 1905–)

John Harvey *Victorian Novelists and Their Illustrators* (Sidgwick & Jackson, 1970)

Oxford Reader's Companion to Dickens, edited by Paul Schlicke
(Oxford University Press, 2000)

Robert L. Patten *Charles Dickens and His Publishers* (Oxford University Press, 1978)

Michael Slater *Dickens and Women* (J. M. Dent, 1983)

Kathleen Tillotson *Novels of the Eighteen Forties* (Oxford University Press, 1954)

Angus Wilson *The World of Charles Dickens* (Secker & Warburg, 1970)

✒ *Index*

Acknowledgements

This book could not have been written without the generations of scholars, editors and biographers who have done so much to make Dickens's work accessible: to them, and especially to those who have so generously shared their knowledge and enthusiasm with me, I owe an enormous debt of gratitude. I should also like to thank Florian Schweizer and the staff of the Charles Dickens Museum, and Andrew Russell of the Victoria and Albert Museum, for their unfailing kindness and courtesy in allowing me access to the collections in their care. Finally I should like to thank my editors and colleagues Lara Speicher, Charlotte Lochhead and Kathleen Houghton for their invaluable help, advice and support.

The British Library is grateful to the Charles Dickens Museum, London, the Victoria and Albert Museum, the Trustees of the National Portrait Gallery, the Free Library of Philadelphia, the Guildhall Library, the British Museum, Portsmouth County Council, the Centre for Kentish Studies, Canterbury, and other named copyright holders for permission to reproduce illustrations.

Front cover illustrations: Page from a fragment, consisting of twenty-two leaves, of the manuscript of *Nicholas Nickleby* (The British Library, Add. MS 57493, f.1); Charles Dickens in 1867 by Ben Gurney (The British Library, Dex. 316); Street scene, 1837 from *Her Majesty's Glorious Jubilee*, 1897 published by the *Illustrated London News* (The British Library, Cup.1264.d.9)

Back cover illustration: Gad's Hill (The British Library 10347.d.1/12); Charles Dickens by Herbert Watkins in 1859. (The British Library, Dex.316)

Half-title page: Charles Dickens by Daniel Maclise, 1839. The portrait commissioned by Dickens's publishers Chapman and Hall and presented to him at the 'Nickleby' dinner held to celebrate the completion of the novel on 5 October 1839. (National Portrait Gallery)

Frontispiece: The opening of Fanny Squeers's letter from chapter 15 of *Nicholas Nickleby*. (The British Library, Add. MS 57493, f.8)

Contents page: Whitechapel High Street by T. H. Shepherd (*c.* 1828), described in *Pickwick Papers* as a 'pretty densely populated quarter' of crowded streets lined with oyster-stalls. (Mary Evans Picture Library)

Published in the United States of America by
Oxford University Press Inc.
198 Madison Avenue
New York, NY 10016
www.oup.com

Oxford is a registered trademark of Oxford University Press Inc.
Library of Congress Cataloging-in-Publication data is available.

ISBN 0-19-521788-8

First published in 2004 by The British Library, 96 Euston Road, London NW1 2DB

Designed and typeset by Crayon Design, Stoke Row, Henley-on-Thames
Map by John Mitchell
Colour and black-and-white origination by South Sea International Press
Printed in Hong Kong by South Sea International Press